FANTASTIC, FASCINATING AND FACTUAL

Robert Ripley's personally trained staff reaches out to the most remote corners of the world to unearth strange, wonderful, tantalizing facts. Here is another eye-opening collection—vividly narrated, graphically illustrated, and absolutely authenticated.

If you cannot buy your favorite **BELIEVE IT OR NOT! POCKET BOOK** at your local newsstand, please write to the nearest Ripley's "Believe It or Not!" museum:

175 Jefferson Street, San Francisco, California 94133

1500 North Wells Street, Chicago, Illinois 60610

19 San Marco Avenue, St. Augustine, Florida 32084

The Parkway, Gatlinburg, Tennessee 37738

145 East Elkhorn Avenue, Estes Park, Colorado 80517

4960 Clifton Hill, Niagara Falls, Canada

Central Promenade, Blackpool, Lancashire, England

RIPLEY'S BELIEVE IT OR NOT! 12th Series is an original POCKET BOOK edition.

Published by POCKET BOOKS

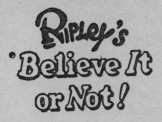

Ripley's Believe It or Not!

12th Series

PUBLISHED BY POCKET BOOKS NEW YORK

RIPLEY'S BELIEVE IT OR NOT!® 12TH SERIES

POCKET BOOK edition published September, 1966
3rd printing......................January, 1974

This original POCKET BOOK edition is printed from
brand-new plates made from newly set, clear, easy-to-read
type. POCKET BOOK editions are published by
POCKET BOOKS, a division of Simon & Schuster,
Inc., 630 Fifth Avenue, New York, N.Y. 10020.
Trademarks registered in the United States
and other countries.

L

PREFACE

About 150 years ago John Lawson of Penicuik, Scotland, looking for a wife, wooed many girls. He always tested their temper by tossing them fully dressed into the nearest river. This BELIEVE IT OR NOT! cartoon promptly brought a query from a lady in Ohio. She was interested in the item because John Lawson was her great-grandfather!

Some years ago we introduced the story of a Mexican state governor who became curious about the number of illegitimate children with a claim on his paternity. He opened offices in all the towns of the state for the express purpose of registering any such claimants. The total ran to many hundreds.

A very charming lady, the wife of a prominent American educator, took it from here. It appeared that she was the only legitimate child of the Mexican governor. The revelation was a stunning surprise to her. She had never even suspected it. We forwarded to her a photostat copy of a four-column front page of a Mexican newspaper that told the story.

Alessandro Guidi, an Italian poet and author, died in 1712 of a typographical error. In the first copy of a Latin book he authored he found a single misspelled word. The vexation promptly killed him. Within a few days after our cartoon appeared, the librarian of an American ecclesiastical institution informed us that the very book which was so fatal to Guidi two and a half centuries ago, was on his library shelves!

A book could be written about these coincidental results that occur practically every week. They are extremely stimulating to us, proving the universality and reach of our feature.

It is on this note that we launch this, the twelfth collection of BELIEVE IT OR NOT! May it continue to enchant those who are animated by a natural human curiosity as well as those who discover a familiar name among its subjects.

As in the past, we are prepared to authenticate every statement in this edition, and all of the illustrations, which were supervised by our distinguished Art Director Paul Frehm.

—Norbert Pearlroth
Research Director
Ripley's BELIEVE IT OR NOT!

THE **COVERED BRIDGE** of North Blenheim, N.Y., A SPAN OF 210 FEET OVER THE SCHOHARIE CREEK, WAS ORIGINALLY CONSTRUCTED ON DRY LAND -THEN TAKEN APART AND REASSEMBLED OVER THE CREEK WHERE IT ENDURED FOR 109 YEARS

THE **SOFT FELT HAT** WAS INTRODUCED IN THE UNITED STATES IN 1851 BY LAJOS KOSSUTH, THE HUNGARIAN FREEDOM FIGHTER, WHO WAS SO POPULAR AMERICANS ADOPTED HIS HEADGEAR

A **HOUSE** in Lafayette, La., BEQUEATHED BY ANDREW SELLERS TO HIS 2 SONS, WAS CUT INTO 2 HALVES WHICH WERE MOVED APART SO EACH COULD ENJOY A SEPARATE INHERITANCE

THE **ROYAL HOSPITAL**
in London, England,
WAS CONSTRUCTED BY TAXING
EVERY MEMBER OF ENGLAND'S
ARMED FORCES ONE DAY'S PAY
(1690)

THE **BELLS** of the Church
of Jever, Germany,
WERE ORDERED RUNG NIGHTLY IN
1575 TO GUIDE HOME THE CITY'S
75-YEAR-OLD RULER, MARIA, WHO
HAD MYSTERIOUSLY DISAPPEARED—
*THEY HAVE BEEN RUNG EVERY
NIGHT FOR 389 YEARS*

**POMPEO
COLONNA**
(1479-1532)
of Naples, Italy,
DIED AFTER
EATING AS
A DESSERT
*12 POUNDS
OF SMYRNA
FIGS*

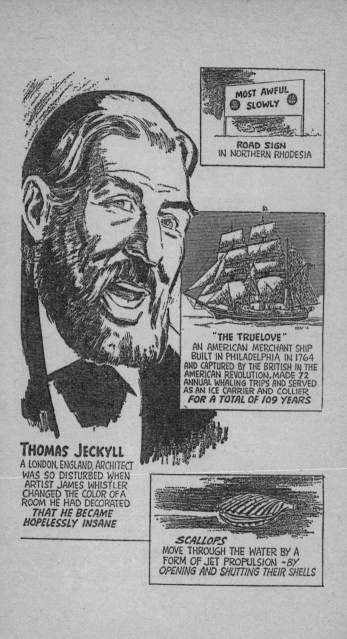

MOST AWFUL SLOWLY

ROAD SIGN
IN NORTHERN RHODESIA

"THE TRUELOVE"
AN AMERICAN MERCHANT SHIP
BUILT IN PHILADELPHIA IN 1764
AND CAPTURED BY THE BRITISH IN THE
AMERICAN REVOLUTION, MADE 72
ANNUAL WHALING TRIPS AND SERVED
AS AN ICE CARRIER AND COLLIER
FOR A TOTAL OF 109 YEARS

THOMAS JECKYLL

A LONDON, ENGLAND, ARCHITECT
WAS SO DISTURBED WHEN
ARTIST JAMES WHISTLER
CHANGED THE COLOR OF A
ROOM HE HAD DECORATED
*THAT HE BECAME
HOPELESSLY INSANE*

SCALLOPS
MOVE THROUGH THE WATER BY A
FORM OF JET PROPULSION –BY
OPENING AND SHUTTING THEIR SHELLS

COL. SIR WILLIAM HUDDLESTON
(1603 - 1668)
WAS ONE OF 9 BROTHERS
—ALL OF WHOM SERVED AS COLONELS
IN THE ARMY OF KING CHARLES I
DURING THE ENGLISH CIVIL WAR

AN **ANCIENT PUNIC TOMB**
in Antioca, Sardinia,
*HAS BEEN CONVERTED
INTO A DWELLING—*
ITALIAN AUTHORITIES
HAVE EVEN GIVEN IT
AN OFFICIAL ADDRESS
—THE NUMBER 77

MRS. LEOLA INGLES
of Cedar Rapids, Iowa,
INJURED IN AN AUTOMOBILE
ACCIDENT IN 1932, CARRIED A
TRIANGLE OF GLASS NEARLY
2" LONG IN HER THIGH
*WITHOUT BEING AWARE OF
ITS PRESENCE FOR 32 YEARS*

CAPT. WILLIAM BRYANT (1694-1772)
MASTER OF THE
MERCHANT SHIP, "JOSEPH,"
*COMPLETED 55 ROUND TRIPS
BETWEEN NEW YORK AND LONDON
NEARLY 200 YEARS AGO*

A MASON'S TROWEL
IMBEDDED IN THE WALL OF
A HOTEL IN NEWARK, OHIO,
IS A MEMORIAL MARKING
THE SPOT FROM WHICH A
*MASON PLUNGED TO HIS
DEATH DURING THE
BUILDING'S CONSTRUCTION*

A PAIR OF
WRENS
THAT BUILT
A NEST
In Cornwall,
England,
*IN THE
SKELETON OF
A PHEASANT*

THE **OFFICIAL MACE** of the Parliament of FIJI **IS THE WAR CLUB WIELDED BY KING THAKOMBAU** *WHEN THE ISLAND WAS POPULATED BY CANNIBALS*

THE **FIRST HOT HOUSE FOR FLOWERS** A CONSERVATORY in Chatsworth, England, 277 FEET LONG, 123 FEET WIDE, AND 67 FEET HIGH, WAS BUILT WITH A CARRIAGE ROAD RUNNING THROUGH IT, SO IT COULD *BE INSPECTED IN 1843 BY THE QUEEN*

THE **WALKING PEPPER SHAKER** FRANZ HAYDINGER OWNER OF AN INN in Vienna, Austria, NEVER PERMITTED PATRONS TO SEASON THEIR OWN FOOD, BUT ON DEMAND WOULD SPRINKLE GROUND PEPPER *WHICH HE ALWAYS CARRIED IN HIS VEST POCKET*

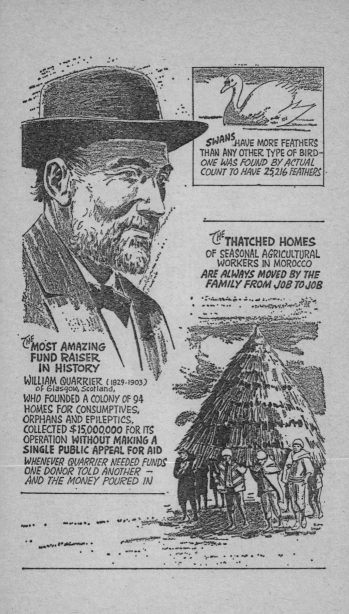

SWANS HAVE MORE FEATHERS THAN ANY OTHER TYPE OF BIRD— ONE WAS FOUND BY ACTUAL COUNT TO HAVE 25,216 FEATHERS

THE THATCHED HOMES OF SEASONAL AGRICULTURAL WORKERS IN MOROCCO ARE ALWAYS MOVED BY THE FAMILY FROM JOB TO JOB

THE MOST AMAZING FUND RAISER IN HISTORY

WILLIAM QUARRIER (1829-1903) of Glasgow, Scotland, WHO FOUNDED A COLONY OF 94 HOMES FOR CONSUMPTIVES, ORPHANS AND EPILEPTICS, COLLECTED $15,000,000 FOR ITS OPERATION WITHOUT MAKING A SINGLE PUBLIC APPEAL FOR AID

WHENEVER QUARRIER NEEDED FUNDS ONE DONOR TOLD ANOTHER — AND THE MONEY POURED IN

Stephen E. Cummings of Norway, Me., IS THE 10TH BOY NAMED STEPHEN TO BE BORN IN THE CUMMINGS FAMILY IN NEW ENGLAND *IN 10 SUCCESSIVE GENERATIONS COVERING A PERIOD OF 300 YEARS*

A **PAGODA** 7 STORIES HIGH LOCATED IN THE IMPERIAL HUNTING-PALACE, Peiping, China, *IS BUILT ENTIRELY OF BLUE PORCELAIN*

DANIEL MANNING (1828-1921) CATTLE DROVER of Watson, Tenn., HANDLED IN EACH HERD HUNDREDS OF ANIMALS FROM MANY FARMS—*YET HE NEVER KEPT A WRITTEN RECORD IN HIS ENTIRE LIFETIME OF 93 YEARS*— THE WEIGHT OF EACH ANIMAL, THE PRICE HE RECEIVED FOR IT AFTER DRIVING THE HERD TO MARKET IN VIRGINIA, AND THE OWNER *WERE ALWAYS MEMORIZED*

THE **ROYAL PALACE** of Mogador, Morocco, BUILT IN 1780 BY A FRENCH ENGINEER NAMED CORNUT, WAS ENGULFED IN THE SANDS OF THE DESERT 35 YEARS LATER — *ON THE VERY DAY CORNUT DIED IN DISTANT FRANCE*

MRS. MARY SPEAR of Scarborough, Me., PICKED 120 QUARTS OF BLUEBERRIES IN THE SUMMER OF 1884 *WHEN SHE WAS 94 YEARS OF AGE*

A **MURDER** BY AN AUSTRALIAN ABORIGINE, CALLED "BAD MEDICINE," WAS REVEALED WHEN FOOTPRINTS LED TO DISCOVERY OF A SKELETON — *THE REMAINS OF A VICTIM WHO HAD BEEN BURIED UPRIGHT IN AN ANTHILL*

DUKE LUDWIG VIII, ruler of Hessen, Germany, FOR A PERIOD OF 35 YEARS ALWAYS TRAVELED IN A CARRIAGE DRAWN *BY 6 STAGS*

The **TOWN** HALL of Newtown, Conn., *NEVER COST THE COMMUNITY A CENT TO BUILD OR TO MAINTAIN* A LOCAL PHILANTHROPIST, MARY HAWLEY, CONSTRUCTED IT FOR $750,000 AND DONATED AN ADDITIONAL $250,000 TO COVER ITS OPERATING EXPENSES

André-Marie AMPÈRE (1775-1836) FRENCH PHYSICIST WHO GAVE HIS NAME TO THE AMPERE, WAS REFUSED A BOOK ON MATHEMATICS BY A LIBRARIAN BECAUSE IT WAS PRINTED IN LATIN *-SO HE MASTERED LATIN IN 2 MONTHS AT THE AGE OF 8!*

OPTICAL ILLUSION
THE IRON GATE of Clementinum College, in Prague, Czechoslovakia, APPEARS TO BE RECESSED IN THE CENTER —*YET ACTUALLY IT IS PERFECTLY FLAT*

NICCOLO FONTANA (1506-1559)
WHO BECAME ONE OF THE FOREMOST MATHEMATICIANS OF ALL TIME, WAS SO POOR THAT AT THE AGE OF 6 HE PRACTICED HIS NUMBERS IN A CEMETERY - *USING TOMBSTONES AS SLATES*

Celtic CAVALRYMEN
DURING THE ROMAN OCCUPATION OF BRITAIN, WORE HELMETS LIKE THOSE OF THEIR CONQUERORS — AND
ADDED FACE MASKS TO MAKE THEM LOOK ROMAN

A CITY GATE
In Ayassoluk, Turkey,
BUILT BY THE GREEKS 1,600
YEARS AGO, WAS CONSTRUCTED
*OUT OF TOMBSTONES
AND COFFIN LIDS*

RATS LIVE ON
NO EVIL STAR
SENTENCE THAT
READS THE SAME
FORWARD AND
BACKWARD

THE DEVIL FISH
of Africa
IS SO
TERRIFYING
IN APPEARANCE
THAT PARENTS
USE IT AS
THE "BOGY"
*TO FRIGHTEN
DISOBEDIENT
CHILDREN*

ANNE KEITH (1639 - 1772)
of Newnham, England,
AT THE AGE OF 133 DECIDED TO
DISTRIBUTE HER ESTATE OF
$30,000 AMONG HER 3 DAUGHTERS
THE YOUNGEST OF WHOM WAS 109

THE DESERT HUTS THAT PROVIDE BREAKFAST IN BED

BEDOUINS BUILD THEIR HOMES IN THE SAHARA AROUND A LIVE DATE PALM —*AND EACH MORNING FIND ON THEIR BED SUFFICIENT FRUIT FOR THEIR MORNING MEAL*

ALEXANDER DUMAS
(1802-1870)
celebrated French novelist
BECAUSE HE ALWAYS WALKED ON TIPTOES AS A CHILD AND SEEMED ABOUT TO SOAR AWAY *WAS FORCED BY HIS MOTHER TO WEAR SHOES OF SOLID IRON*

THE ELEPHANT'S HEAD
NATURAL STONE FORMATION
near Las Vegas, Nev.

BONALY TOWER in Scotland OVERLOOKS 8 DIFFERENT COUNTIES.

The MISER TO WHOM MONEY MEANT MORE THAN HIS LIFE

THE 2d EARL OF LINCOLN (1540-1616) ORDERED BY QUEEN ELIZABETH I TO ENTERTAIN HER AT DINNER *RISKED EXECUTION FOR SNUBBING HER MAJESTY BY CONCEALING HIMSELF AND KEEPING THE* GATES OF HIS MANSION LOCKED

The FRONDS of THE CINNAMON FERN *LOOK LIKE SHEPHERDS' CROOKS*

WRECKAGE OF THE STEAM FREIGHTER "NICARAGUA" WHICH RAN AGROUND off Padre, Texas, IN 1912 *IS STILL IN THE SAME SPOT 52 YEARS LATER*

THE **OFFICIAL STAFF** OF THE MAYOR OF Nova Ves, Czechoslovakia, IS CARVED IN THE SHAPE OF A HUMAN HAND—*WITH THE INDEX FINGER AND THUMB CURVED IN THE CHARACTERISTIC AMERICAN SIGN FOR "OK"*

SA'DI
(1184-1292)
THE FAMED PERSIAN POET VOWED AT 18 TO DIVIDE HIS FUTURE INTO 3 EQUAL PERIODS –30 YEARS FOR AN EDUCATION, 30 YEARS FOR TRAVEL, AND 30 YEARS FOR RETIREMENT—
HE DIED AT THE AGE OF 108 ON THE LAST DAY OF HIS THIRD 30-YEAR PERIOD

2 STORKS
RETURNED FOR 3 SUCCESSIVE YEARS
to their nests near Dresden, Germany
- *APPARENTLY UNHAMPERED BY ARROWS THAT HAD PENETRATED THEIR BODIES*
(1908-1910)

DR. BENJAMIN THOMAS
President of Judson University, Judsonia, Ark.,
WAS ONE OF 5 BROTHERS
- *ALL OF WHOM WERE PREACHERS*

THE **ATTORNEY** WHOSE DEFENSE WAS TOO PERFECT!

CLEMENT VALLANDIGHAM (1820-1871)
DEFENDING AN ACCUSED MURDERER
in Lebanon, Ohio,
PLEDGED IN HIS OPENING STATEMENT TO THE JURY THAT HE WOULD PROVE THAT IF HIS CLIENT HAD HANDLED THE GUN IN THE MANNER CHARGED
HE WOULD HAVE KILLED HIMSELF!

PRACTICING WITH A LOADED REVOLVER IN FRONT OF A MIRROR ON THE EVE OF HIS SUMMATION ADDRESS, VALLANDIGHAM *ACCIDENTALLY KILLED HIMSELF* (June 17, 1871)

GEORGE REEVES-SMITH
(1860-1941)
WAS CONSIDERED SO
COMPETENT A HOTEL
MAN THAT WHEN THE
OWNERS OF LONDON'S
SAVOY HOTEL FOUND
HE COULD NOT MANAGE
THEIR HOTEL BECAUSE
OF A CONTRACT
WITH THE BERKELEY
-*THEY BOUGHT THE
BERKELEY HOTEL* (1900)

THE **TOWER** of the CRIMINAL COURT,
in HOBART, AUSTRALIA,
FORMERLY SERVED AS THE
TOWER OF THE CITY CHURCH

THE **OLIVE
SHELL**
a mollusk
ACTUALLY
RESEMBLES
AN OLIVE

**THE OLDEST SCHOOL "BOOK"
IN THE WORLD**
A CLAY TABLET found in Syria
AND ENGRAVED IN THE
ANCIENT UGARIT ALPHABET
*WAS USED AS A PRIMER
BY A YOUNG STUDENT
3,300 YEARS AGO*

THE **CHAPEL OF ST. NICHOLAS**
in Calw, Germany,
IS LOCATED IN A
BRIDGE PILLAR OVER
THE NAGOLD RIVER
-AND HAS BEEN USED
FOR RELIGIOUS SERVICES
FOR 564 YEARS

MARIE ROBIE
of Wollaston, Mass.,
PLAYING AT THE FURNACE
BROOK GOLF CLUB
SCORED AN ACE ON
THE FIRST HOLE
-WHICH MEASURES
393 YARDS

CALIPH OMAR I
WHO RULED THE
MOHAMMEDAN WORLD
FROM 634 TO 644
CONQUERED 36,000
COMMUNITIES
-AND DESTROYED 14,000
PLACES OF WORSHIP

MOUNT SNAEFELL
HIGHEST SPOT ON THE ISLE OF MAN,
HAS AN ELEVATION OF ONLY 2,034 FEET
-YET IT OFFERS A VIEW OF ENGLAND,
SCOTLAND, WALES, IRELAND, THE ISLE
OF MAN AND THE ISLAND OF LUNDY

QUADRUPLET
PECAN

SPECIAL EATING POTS
WHICH CANNOT BE
FILLED SIMULTANEOUSLY
ARE USED BY TWINS
in Dahomey, Africa,
*BECAUSE THEY ARE
FORBIDDEN TO
EAT TOGETHER*

JOHANN SEGER of Vaduz, Liechtenstein,
HAD A FULL SET OF TEETH WHEN HE DIED AT THE AGE OF 93
HE HAD LOST ONE OF HIS PERMANENT TEETH-AT THE AGE OF 80-
BUT GREW A NEW ONE TO REPLACE IT

MAYOR HENRY GAPE of St. Albans, England, WHO SERVED IN THAT POST IN 1554 WAS SUCCEEDED IN OFFICE BY **16 DIRECT DESCENDANTS**—*MEMBERS OF HIS FAMILY SERVED AS MAYORS CONTINUOUSLY FOR 265 YEARS*

PHILIP GRABINSKI IN A LUMBER CAMP near Kapowsin, Wash., CLIMBED TO THE TOP OF A 150-FOOT TREE AND DESCENDED AGAIN TO THE GROUND *IN ONE MINUTE, 21 SECONDS* 1915

MOZART   NORMAL

THE **EARS of MOZART** the Austrian composer HAD OPENINGS *TWICE THE SIZE OF NORMAL EARS*

THE MEMORIAL TO AN IDEA

6 STONE SEATS LINE THE CITY WALL OF Neutsch, Germany, BUILT IN THE 18th CENTURY **FOR THE JURISTS OF A TAX COURT THAT WAS NEVER CREATED** – *THE SEATS ARE A MEMORIAL TO THE ABANDONED PLAN*

CARDBOARD CUT-OUTS

DEPICTING SERVANTS CARRYING TEACUPS ARE BURNED AT CHINESE FUNERALS IN THE BELIEF THAT THE SPIRITS OF THE SERVANTS *WILL ATTEND THE DEPARTED IN THE NEXT WORLD*

ANN ROBINS (1702-1810)

BECAME SEXTON AND "HANDYMAN" of the Church of Newnham, England, WHEN SHE WAS 84 YEARS OF AGE AND WORKED DAILY AT THE TWO JOBS UNTIL SHE *REACHED THE AGE OF 107*

THE MOSQUE of **SULTAN HASSAN** in Cairo, Egypt, COMPLETED IN 1362, *WAS BUILT WITH STONES STRIPPED FROM THE GREAT PYRAMID*

THE **FRUIT** of the Barbados Gooseberry **BEARS LEAVES**

FASHION LEADERS— THE SANDALS WORN BY CHIC GREEK LADIES of Alexandria, Egypt, IN THE 2d CENTURY B.C. *HAD IMBEDDED IN THEIR SOLES NAILHEADS WHICH SPELLED OUT THE GREEK WORD "AKOLOIEI"* WHICH MEANS *"FOLLOW ME"*

AKOLOYOI

WILLIAM HOLDEN (1818-1892) of Hillsborough, N.C., BECAME GOVERNOR OF NORTH CAROLINA AND EDITOR OF A RALEIGH NEWSPAPER – YET WHEN HE WAS A PRINTER'S APPRENTICE AT THE AGE OF 16 AND LEFT HIS JOB WITHOUT PERMISSION, A REWARD OF *ONLY 5 CENTS WAS OFFERED FOR HIS RETURN*

A MECHANIZED GOLD EXCAVATOR
WAS USED IN THE DOMINION CREEK
VALLEY OF THE CANADIAN KLONDIKE
FOR JUST 2 MINUTES - AND
THEN ABANDONED AS
IMPRACTICAL ALTHOUGH
IT HAD COST ITS OWNER,
ARTHUR THREADGOLD,
$500,000

WILLARD G. WATERS
of Randallstown, Maryland,
SCORED A 79 at the Country Club
of Maryland
AT THE AGE OF 89

JULIA TYLER
WIFE OF PRESIDENT JOHN TYLER
REGARDED THE ANNEXATION OF
TEXAS HER HUSBAND'S GREATEST
ACHIEVEMENT AND WORE THE
GOLD PEN HE USED CLOSE TO HER
HEART BENEATH HER CLOTHING
EVERY DAY FOR 44 YEARS

SCALLOPS BY ALTERNATELY OPENING AND CLOSING THEIR VALVES, FLIT THROUGH THE WATER BY A FORM OF JET PROPULSION

"AND'" a town between Stein and Krems in Austria WAS SO NAMED BY A PUZZLE-LOVING RULER WHO WOULD ASK, "HOW MANY TOWNS ARE STEIN AND KREMS?" THE CORRECT ANSWER WAS 3

OPTICAL ILLUSION

THE REV. MANASSEH CUTLER (1742-1823) ONE OF THE FOUNDERS OF OHIO WAS A DOCTOR OF LAW A DOCTOR OF DIVINITY AND A DOCTOR OF MEDICINE

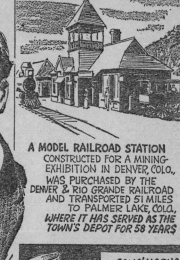

A MODEL RAILROAD STATION
CONSTRUCTED FOR A MINING
EXHIBITION IN DENVER, COLO.,
WAS PURCHASED BY THE
DENVER & RIO GRANDE RAILROAD
AND TRANSPORTED 51 MILES
TO PALMER LAKE, COLO.,
*WHERE IT HAS SERVED AS THE
TOWN'S DEPOT FOR 58 YEARS*

COWS' HORNS
WITH A HOLE
DRILLED IN THE
END WERE USED
in medieval England
*AS BABIES'
NURSING
BOTTLES*

**DR. JOHN
BLACKWOOD**
(1775-1840)
of Mount Holly, N.J.,
WAS A WEALTHY
PHYSICIAN, JUDGE
AND POSTMASTER
*-YET HE NEVER OWNED
MORE THAN ONE SHIRT*
WHILE HIS SHIRT WAS
BEING LAUNDERED
HE STAYED IN BED

TURKHEN
A
CROSS
BETWEEN A
TURKEY
AND A
CHICKEN

"MOUCHE"
A POODLE OWNED BY
THE LAYARD FAMILY
of Florence, Italy,
WAS SO TERRIFIED OF
THE DARK THAT HE
WOULD NOT LEAVE
THE HOUSE AT NIGHT
*UNLESS A LIGHTED
LANTERN WAS HUNG
FROM HIS NECK*

THE
PULPIT
of the
Church of
Villingen,
Germany,
CONSISTING
OF
INTRICATE
CARVINGS
*WAS
CREATED BY
A BLIND
MAN* (1500)

THE **MOST**
PERSISTENT
BILL COLLECTOR
IN HISTORY
—
JOE DUN
bailiff of Lincoln, England,
WAS SO TENACIOUS IN TRAILING
DOWN DEBTORS THAT HIS NAME
BECAME PROVERBIAL
I.E. – TO "DUN" A MAN

NAPOLEON BONAPARTE
in the Battle of Aucis-sur-Aube, France,
AS AN EXAMPLE OF COURAGE FOR HIS GREEN
TROOPS CAUSED HIS HORSE "ROITELET" TO
STRADDLE AN UNEXPLODED ARTILLERY SHELL—
THE SHELL EXPLODED AND BLEW NAPOLEON
AND HIS MOUNT A DISTANCE OF 60 FEET
**-YET BOTH HORSE AND RIDER
ESCAPED WITHOUT INJURY**

**WOLF ROCK
LIGHTHOUSE**
OFF THE COAST OF
Cornwall, England,
CUT OFF FROM
SUPPLIES BY ROUGH
SEAS FOR 25 DAYS,
WAS DELIVERED
FOOD FROM A
STORM-TOSSED SHIP
*BY MEANS OF A
KITE MADE FROM
AN OLD FLOUR BAG*
(1952)

**THE REV.
WILL SCHULTZ**
of Izard County, Ark.,
MEMORIZED EVERY
WORD OF THE BIBLE

MRS. **CHRISTOPHER COLUMBUS SIMMON** WAS MARRIED IN Seattle, Wash., IN A CEREMONY PERFORMED BY THE REV. DANIEL BAGLEY *WHEN SHE WAS ONLY 13 YEARS OF AGE—* A WITNESS ASSURED THE CLERGYMAN THE BRIDE WAS "OVER 18," BUT LATER EXPLAINED THAT HE HAD PREPARED FOR A QUERY ABOUT THE GIRL'S AGE BY *HAVING HER PUT THE NUMBER "18" IN EACH OF HER SHOES*

THE MASONRY COFFIN OF A LADY BURIED IN REGGIO, ITALY, AND EXCAVATED 2,300 YEARS LATER *WAS IN THE SHAPE OF A SCULPTURED FOOT AND SANDAL*

2 WILD BOARS WERE TRAINED BY FRANÇOIS BOUCHAYEZ, FAMED FRENCH SPORTSMAN, *TO SERVE AS "HUNTING DOGS"*

THE FIRST "AIRPLANE"
Sierra Mahoma Range, Uruguay
NATURAL STONE FORMATION
1,000,000 YEARS OLD

MUSICIANS
in Bolivia
PLAY
REED
PIPES
TALLER
THAN
THEMSELVES

ALLIGATORS
DROWN
IF HELD
UNDER
WATER

WE SELL THE WORST WHISKY & CIGARS

SIGN In Georgetown, Colo., MADE FOR AN ILLITERATE SALOONKEEPER BY A SIGNPAINTER WHO HATED HIM —YET, THE SIGN MADE THE SALOON AN IMMEDIATE SUCCESS

JOSEF JLL (1809-1885) VILLAGE SURGEON OF Steisslingen, Austria, WAS THE 8th GENERATION OF HIS FAMILY TO FILL THAT POST *DURING A CONSECUTIVE PERIOD OF 245 YEARS*

ANIMAL SKINS In Morocco ARE STRIPPED OF THEIR HAIR BEFORE TANNING BY SPREADING THEM ON BUSY THOROUGHFARES *SO THAT THE HAIR IS WORN AWAY BY THE FEET OF PASSERSBY*

THE SKELETON BRIDGE OF LAKE BAGOE
Africa
A BRIDGE, USED REGULARLY BY
NATIVE TRAVELERS, CONSISTS
ONLY OF ROUGH TREE TRUNKS
— WITH A GAP OF SEVERAL FEET
BETWEEN EACH TRUNK

Alexandre
COLIN
(1798-1875)
CELEBRATED FRENCH PAINTER
WAS THE *HUSBAND* OF A PAINTER
THE *NEPHEW* OF 6 PAINTERS
THE *BROTHER* OF 2 PAINTERS
THE *FATHER* OF 4 PAINTERS
THE *FATHER-IN-LAW* OF 3 PAINTERS
and
GRANDFATHER OF 4 PAINTERS

THE ALUMINUM STATUE of MUSSOLINI
STILL STANDS IN
WAIDBRUCK, ITALY

EDWARD D. BAKER
(1811-1861)
WAS A NATIVE OF LONDON, ENGLAND,
SERVED AS A CONGRESSMAN FROM
ILLINOIS FROM 1845 TO 1851,
*AND A U.S. SENATOR FROM
OREGON IN 1859 AND 1860*

THE **TOWER**
CLOCK of VITTORIOSA
on the island of Malta
**HAS BEEN RUNNING
WITHOUT INTERRUPTION**
FOR 433 YEARS

THE **EAGLE RAY**
of the Mediterranean,
WHICH HAS A HIGHLY POISONOUS STING IN ITS TAIL,
LOOKS REMARKABLY LIKE A SOARING EAGLE

THE SACRED
ICICLE OF KASHMIR
*A HUGE ICICLE
10 FEET HIGH
LOCATED IN THE
CAVE OF AMARNATH
IS VISITED
ANNUALLY BY HUNDREDS OF
THOUSANDS OF PILGRIMS
WHO CLIMB 15,600 FEET
TO PAY IT HOMAGE*

ADAM
SKIRVING
of Clackmae, Scotland,
A FARMER ESCAPING FROM
BRITISH TROOPS IN 1745
*COVERED A DISTANCE
OF 61½ FEET IN 3 LEAPS*

27 PINE CONES
GROWING IN A CLUSTER
ON ONE STEM

THE FRAMEWORK OF THE ROSE WINDOW in the Church of La Sainte Chapélle, Paris, **35 FEET HIGH AND 38 FEET WIDE** *WAS CUT FROM ONE ROCK* (1485)

FLUTES USED BY THE Timbiras Indians of Brazil ARE MADE OUT OF *2 HUMAN THIGHBONES*

GENERAL FRANÇOIS de FAVRAT (1710-1792) SERVED DURING HIS MILITARY CAREER AS A CAPTAIN IN THE SPANISH, FRENCH, SARDINIAN, SAXON AND AUSTRIAN ARMIES, AND AS A PRUSSIAN GENERAL— FOUGHT IN 84 BATTLES AND WAS WOUNDED 14 TIMES —4 TIMES AS A GENERAL

THE FERRY on Lake Larne, Ireland, BETWEEN LARNE AND ISLAND MAGEE, INAUGURATED BY ST. PATRICK, HAS NEVER HAD A DROWNING IN 1,500 YEARS

A BLACKSMITH SHOP in St. Clement Danes, England, UNDER A LEASE GRANTED BY KING HENRY II HAS PAID AN ANNUAL RENTAL OF 6 HORSESHOES AND 61 NAILS FOR 804 YEARS

JOSEPH GUYERMELLI A LOGGER AT KETCHIKAN, ALASKA, FELL 125 FEET FROM A TREE AND SUFFERED ONLY A BROKEN LEG

GREEN SMITH (1800-1915)
of Holly Leaf, Tenn.,
LIVED IN THE SAME
LOG CABIN FOR
100 YEARS

PETITIONS
OF
Collar and Cuff
AND
SHIRT OPERATIVES

THE
LARGEST
PETITION
EVER
PRESENTED
TO
CONGRESS

IT WEIGHED 580 POUNDS AND
CONTAINED 70,000 SIGNATURES
1894

BARON
PHILIP von
STOSCH
(1691-1747) A GERMAN
residing in Florence, Italy,
INVENTED THE MONOCLE IN 1727
NOT AS AN ARTICLE OF FASHION
-BUT BECAUSE HE HAD EYES
OF UNEQUAL VISION

A *TOWER* near Neideck, Germany, BUILT AS A MEMORIAL TO AN ANCIENT CASTLE *WAS CONSTRUCTED FROM ITS DEBRIS*

DAVID HAND of Sag Harbor, N.Y., A PRIVATEER DURING THE AMERICAN REVOLUTION *WAS CAPTURED BY THE BRITISH 5 TIMES -ESCAPING EACH TIME*

THE *CITY WALL* of Amelia, Italy, 2,800 FEET LONG, HAS NO CEMENT OR OTHER BINDER -*YET IT HAS ENDURED FOR 3,400 YEARS*

THE **CHURCH** OF **LIPARI** in Italy, LOCATED IN THE SHADOW OF A SMOKING VOLCANO, IS CALLED THE **CHURCH OF PURGATORY**

A **HAND HOLDING A SWORD** IS STILL HUNG ON THE CITY HALL OF Münster, Germany, AS A REMINDER THAT RIOTERS FORMERLY WERE *PUNISHED BY DEATH*

GONCALO EANNES BANDARRA (1500-1556) WAS A SHOEMAKER WHO COULD NEITHER READ NOR WRITE—YET HE BECAME PORTUGAL'S MOST HONORED POET

HIS POETRY, TRANSCRIBED BY FRIENDS, WAS HAILED AS IMMORTAL

THE **FLAG HOUSE** in Baltimore, Md., WHERE MARY PICKERSGILL MADE THE STAR-SPANGLED BANNER THAT INSPIRED FRANCIS SCOTT KEY TO COMPOSE THE NATIONAL ANTHEM, IS THE ONLY HOME AUTHORIZED BY CONGRESS TO FLY BOTH THE NATIONAL FLAG AND THE FLAG OF 1814 *DAY AND NIGHT*

CHARLES CARROLL (1737-1832) of Carrollton, Md., WAS THE ONLY SIGNER OF THE DECLARATION OF INDEPENDENCE *WHO EVER SAW A RAILROAD!*

THE **FAN PALM** (Licuala peltata) EACH OF ITS FAN-SHAPED LEAVES CONSISTS OF *HUNDREDS OF THIN SECTIONS*

THE CASTLE OF SAINT-FARGEAU in France
WAS BESTOWED BY KING CHARLES VII
ON ANTOINE de CHABANNES
-A HIGHWAY ROBBER
CHABANNES WAS GIVEN THE CASTLE
FOR REVEALING A PLOT TO KILL
THE MONARCH *- A CONSPIRACY
HE ACTUALLY INSTIGATED HIMSELF*

NATIVES OF THE **LABI TRIBE** Africa
WEAR NO CLOTHING
-BUT THEY ALWAYS CARRY A PORTABLE SCREEN!

SULTAN OMAR ALI of Brunei, British Borneo,
WOULD HAVE BEEN REFUSED
HIS COUNTRY'S THRONE BECAUSE
HE WAS AN IMBECILE
*-BUT HE WAS INSTALLED AS
SULTAN IN 1828 BECAUSE HE
WAS BORN WITH 2 RIGHT THUMBS*

A CHICKEN COOP near Corrientes, Argentina, WAS ORIGINALLY BUILT AS A WILD-ANIMAL TRAP — AND *ACTUALLY CAPTURED 30 JAGUARS*

THE **GIANT'S HEAD** Hopewell Cape, Canada *NATURAL STONE FORMATION*

ANDRANA of Madura, in Southern India, TO ATONE FOR AN ACT OF DISRESPECT TO HIS TEACHER WALKED FROM HIS HOME TO THE HOLY TOWN OF BADRINATH AND BACK — A DISTANCE OF 3,200 MILES!

HE MADE THE ENTIRE JOURNEY TO BADRINATH BY FALLING TO THE GROUND, RISING AND THEN FALLING AGAIN — AND ON THE RETURN TRIP NEVER ONCE SAT OR RECLINED FOR A PERIOD OF 4 YEARS

OPTICAL ILLUSION

SAN ANTONIO ROAD
WHICH EXTENDS FROM Mexico City to Louisiana and crosses Texas
IS LEGALLY DEFINED AS A NAVIGABLE RIVER SO NO LAND GRANT CAN EXTEND ACROSS IT

GEORGE WASHINGTON
NOT ONLY DID NOT CHOP DOWN A CHERRY TREE
—HE WAS ALLERGIC TO CHERRIES

THE PULPIT of the CATHEDRAL of Freiberg, Germany, IS SHAPED LIKE A TULIP

THE STRANGEST COCKTAIL PARTY IN HISTORY

THE PARTY CELEBRATING COMPLETION OF THE CONSTRUCTION OF THE FRAMEWORK OF A STUFFED ELEPHANT IN THE PARIS, FRANCE, ZOO, WAS ATTENDED BY SEVERAL HUNDRED PERSONS — *—AND HELD INSIDE THE ELEPHANT* (1817)

from an old print

THE ANGLER FISH
IN ADDITION TO THE TEETH IN ITS JAWS HAS TEETH ON THE FLOOR OF ITS MOUTH —*SMALL BIRDS OCCASIONALLY FLY INTO ITS MOUTH AND BECOME STUCK ON THESE TEETH, FROM WHICH THE FISH HAS DIFFICULTY DISLODGING THEM*

JEROME MAGISER
(1553-1618)
FAMED GERMAN STUDENT OF LANGUAGES, AT THE AGE OF 16 COULD REPEAT FROM MEMORY ANY SERMON HE EVER HEARD *—TRANSLATING IT INTO GREEK VERSE*

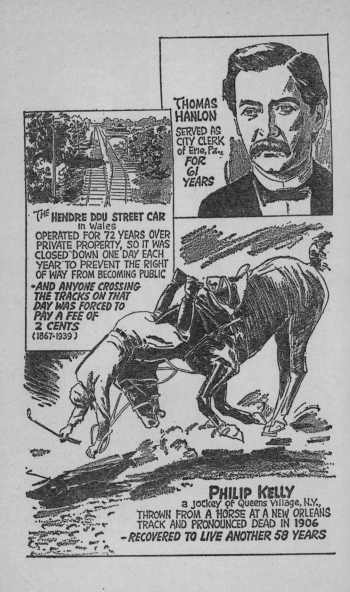

THOMAS HANLON SERVED AS CITY CLERK of Erie, Pa., FOR 61 YEARS

THE HENDRE DDU STREET CAR in Wales OPERATED FOR 72 YEARS OVER PRIVATE PROPERTY, SO IT WAS CLOSED DOWN ONE DAY EACH YEAR TO PREVENT THE RIGHT OF WAY FROM BECOMING PUBLIC

•AND ANYONE CROSSING THE TRACKS ON THAT DAY WAS FORCED TO PAY A FEE OF 2 CENTS (1867-1939)

PHILIP KELLY a jockey of Queens Village, N.Y., THROWN FROM A HORSE AT A NEW ORLEANS TRACK AND PRONOUNCED DEAD IN 1906 -RECOVERED TO LIVE ANOTHER 58 YEARS

THE HEDGE THEATRE in Salzburg, Austria, IN WHICH PERFORMANCES HAVE BEEN STAGED FOR 250 YEARS, USES AS SCENERY *ONLY THE HEDGES OF THE MIRABELL GARDENS*

MUSICAL THORNS IVORY THORNS COVERING AFRICAN FRUIT TREES ARE HOLLOWED OUT BY INSECTS, AND WINDS BLOWING THROUGH THEM CREATE *A MUSICAL CONCERT*

RINTARO KATSU (1826-1899) a Japanese, AT THE AGE OF 16 TRANSCRIBED IN LONGHAND, THREE TIMES, A 500-PAGE DUTCH DICTIONARY AND MEMORIZED 50,000 DUTCH WORDS

THE **MARCO POLO BRIDGE**
at Lukouchiao, China,
1,000 FEET LONG AND 50 FEET
WIDE, HAS 280 CARVED PILLARS,
EACH TOPPED BY A STONE
LION — *YET NO TWO OF
THE LIONS ARE ALIKE*

PASSES WRITTEN IN CODE
WERE ISSUED TO POOR
TRAVELERS BY THE
NOTORIOUS GERMAN
BANDIT SCHINDERHANNES
*TO ASSURE THEM SAFETY
FROM OTHER ROBBERS*

**CHIEF
KAYIJUKA**
of Muhugira Province,
in Rwanda, Africa,
IS HIS COUNTRY'S FOREMOST AUTHORITY
ON ITS HISTORY AND GENEALOGY
•*YET HE HAS BEEN BLIND FOR 58 YEARS*

DAN LeVALLEY
(1847-1937)
of Garfield
County,
Montana

GIVEN
THE
OPPORTUNITY
TO WITHDRAW
HIS FORTUNE
OF $110,000
FROM A
BANK ON
THE DAY BEFORE
IT CLOSED,
TOOK OUT
ONLY $50
AND LEFT THE
BALANCE TO
AID OTHER
DEPOSITORS

—EXPLAINING
THAT AT THE
AGE OF 90
HE DIDN'T
NEED MUCH
MONEY

"PROHASKA"
AN AUSTRIAN WAR DOG
**PARTICIPATED IN 20
BATTLES AND WAS
WOUNDED 3 TIMES**
AFTER ITS DEATH IT
WAS GIVEN THE
PERMANENT GRADE
OF SERGEANT

THE **MONUMENT**
TO THE **MARTYRS**
OF **TOLPUDDLE,**
England,
A MEMORIAL ERECTED IN
HONOR OF 6 FARMHANDS
WHOSE STRIKE AGAINST
WAGES OF $1.44 A WEEK
IN 1834 CAUSED THEM TO
BE DEPORTED TO AUSTRALIA
**AND SENTENCED TO
7 YEARS'
HARD LABOR**

THE MAN WHO TURNED DAY INTO NIGHT
LORD LEVESON-GOWER (1815-1891) of Staffordshire, England, THROUGHOUT MOST OF HIS LIFE SLEPT DAILY FROM 8 A.M. UNTIL 11 P.M., THEN BREAKFASTED, HUNTED OR VISITED HIS FRIENDS, LUNCHED AT 2 A.M. AND ALWAYS ATE HIS DINNER AT 6 A.M.

THE SWAMP SNAIL Paludina vivipara LAYS NO EGGS AS DO OTHER SNAILS — BUT GIVES BIRTH TO LIVE YOUNG

THE HANGING GARDENS OF VENEZUELA INDIANS in the Orinoco forests TO PROTECT THEIR VEGETABLES FROM ANTS AND ANIMALS PLANT THEIR CROPS IN SOIL IN CANOES ON FRAMES HIGH ABOVE THE GROUND

Johann PFEIFFER (1707-1772) of Harbke, Germany, WAS SO DEDICATED A SCHOOLTEACHER THAT HE EXPIRED WHILE HIS STUDENTS *WERE ATTENDING CLASS BESIDE HIS DEATHBED*

DOORKNOCKERS in Morocco ARE MODELED FROM THE HANDS OF THE YOUNGEST GIRL IN THE HOUSEHOLD AS *A PROTECTION AGAINST EVIL*

UPOLO WOMEN in the Congo WEAR THE FAMILY'S ENTIRE SAVINGS IN THE FORM OF A BRASS COIN SHAPED LIKE A COLLAR *WEIGHING UP TO 35 POUNDS*

Tami McMurray
COULD WHISTLE AT THE
AGE OF 9 MONTHS

THE HOTEL de SULLY — Paris, France,
WAS LOST ON THE TURN OF A CARD
BEFORE IT WAS BUILT
THE LOSER HAD TO CONSTRUCT IT FOR THE WINNER
1624

THE WOMEN WHO WANT TO WADDLE LIKE ELEPHANTS
GIRLS of the Kayah Tribe of Burma
REGARD THE GAIT OF THE ELEPHANT AS SO
GRACEFUL THAT THEY WIND 30 POUNDS OF BANDAGES AROUND
THEIR KNEES SO THEY CAN WALK LIKE THE PACHYDERMS

THE TUNES NO WOMEN MAY HEAR

THE VONEBI INDIANS of the central Orinoco region of Venezuela

BY BLOWING INTO A LARGE POT THROUGH WOODEN TUBES, PRODUCE MUSIC THAT WOMEN ARE FORBIDDEN TO OVERHEAR

UNDER PAIN OF DEATH

SOFIA

THE CAPITAL OF COMMUNIST BULGARIA ORIGINALLY WAS NAMED SERDIKA —BUT WAS RENAMED IN HONOR OF *THIS CHURCH OF ST. SOFIA*

THE COPPER WEATHER VANE

OVER THE LIBERTY & CO. STORE IN London, England, IS A 120-LB. REPLICA OF THE MAYFLOWER

PHILIPPE PUTANGES (1820-1880) A MERCHANT OF Paris, France, NAMED HIS 3 SONS **DOCTEUR, PROFESSEUR** and **COLONEL**

DOCTEUR BECAME A PHYSICIAN. PROFESSEUR BECAME A *COLLEGE PROFESSOR* AND COLONEL BECAME AN *ARMY COLONEL*

THE **GHAIBNATH SIVA TEMPLE** LOCATED IN THE MIDDLE OF THE GANGES RIVER, NEAR Sultanganj, India, IS CONSIDERED SO SACRED THAT WORSHIPERS *ARE FORBIDDEN TO APPROACH IT EXCEPT BY SWIMMING*

A **75-WATT BULB** CAN BE ILLUMINATED BY PATTING A CAT ON A COLD DAY *9,200,000,000 TIMES*

AN **OYSTER** found in the Indian Ocean IS SHAPED LIKE THE **COMB OF A ROOSTER**

A **BARROOM** COMPRISING THE SECOND STORY OF A BUILDING IN AUSTIN, PA., WAS SWEPT OFF THE FIRST FLOOR BY A FLOOD AND CARRIED A QUARTER OF A MILE AWAY -YET NOT A SINGLE GLASS OR BOTTLE WAS BROKEN Sept. 1911

PRINCE-ROMUALD GIÉDROYC A RUSSIAN NOBLEMAN WHILE RESIDING IN PARIS, FRANCE, DURING THE FINAL 20 YEARS OF HIS LIFE *ATE 7 DINNERS EVERY DAY*

THE **SNOW BUTTERFLY** (Parnassius) INHABITS THE ALPINE PEAKS -PERPETUALLY FLITTING OVER FIELDS OF ICE AND SNOW

MRS. EXIOR BEAUCHAMP
of Gladstone, Mich.,
BITTEN BY A DOG IN 1924
UNDERWENT SURGERY IN 1963
*FOR REMOVAL OF A DOG'S
TOOTH THAT HAD BEEN
IMBEDDED IN HER KNEE
UNNOTICED FOR 39 YEARS*

BEDOUIN WOMEN
of the Sinai Peninsula, Egypt,
ARE FORBIDDEN TO DANCE
~EXCEPT ON PITCH-DARK
NIGHTS ON WHICH THERE ARE
NO STARS AND NO MOON

THE NESTS
of THE SWIFT
ARE
CONSIDERED
BY THE
CHINESE
*AN EDIBLE
DELICACY*

A HAT BOX
MADE BY COMMANDER
FLOER, CAPTAIN OF
A WHALING SHIP,
FROM FISH BONES
Amrum, Germany

A NEW CHIEF of the TOUBOURIS in Chad, Africa, WAS ALWAYS INAUGURATED BY HAVING HIS CABINET MEMBERS *BEAT HIM FOR AN HOUR WITH CLUBS*

THE MAIN ALTAR of the CHURCH OF SAN CLEMENTE, in Causaria, Italy, WAS ONCE A STONE COFFIN

FENCES in Tibau, Brazil, ARE MADE FROM THE VEINS OF THE LEAVES *OF THE COCONUT PALM*

THE GREAT DITCH
SURROUNDING THE WADDEN ISLANDS
In The Netherlands
FOR YEARS HAD TO BE CROSSED
PART WAY BY RAFT,
PART WAY BY BOAT,
AND THEN IN A WHEELED
HORSE-DRAWN CART

ABRAHAM LINCOLN
WAS THE ONLY PRESIDENT OF THE UNITED STATES
WHO WHILE SERVING AS COMMANDER-IN-CHIEF
ACTUALLY WITNESSED A BATTLE AND
WAS EXPOSED TO ENEMY FIRE
Fort Stevens, Washington, D.C., June 11, 1864

THE **BRIDGE** OF THE **YOUNG LADIES** in Betanzos, Spain, WAS BUILT BY THE KING OF CASTILE FOR THE CALIPH of Cordoba TO CANCEL HIS AGREEMENT TO SEND THE CALIPH **100 FEMALE SLAVES EACH YEAR** (1200)

A **PRIVATE POSTAGE STAMP** DISPLAYING A HISTORY OF THE SPANISH POST OFFICE WAS ISSUED IN JULY, 1881, FOR THE BOOK'S AUTHOR, ANTONIO FERNANDEZ DURO, WHO WAS GIVEN AS HIS WRITING FEE A 6-MONTHS' SUPPLY OF THE STAMPS

CHILDREN in Nepal ARE CARRIED BY THEIR PARENTS *IN BASKETS SLUNG FROM A YOKE*

SVETI STEFAN
A VILLAGE on the Adriatic
coast of Yugoslavia,
WAS BUILT ON A ROCKY
ISLET IN THE 16th CENTURY
BY SELLING THE VALUABLE
CARGO OF A TURKISH
PIRATE SHIP - *THAT
HAD FOUNDERED
ON ITS ROCKS*

John McDONOGH
(1779 - 1850)
NOTORIOUS IN
NEW ORLEANS FOR
HIS STINGINESS,
*BEQUEATHED TO THE
CITY SUFFICIENT
FUNDS TO CONSTRUCT
35 PUBLIC SCHOOLS*

DOMINVS-LEGEM
DAT-VALERIO-SEVERO
EVTROPI-VIVAS

A **LAMP** SHAPED LIKE A SHIP,
SYMBOLIZING THE HOPE FOR A
LONG VOYAGE THROUGH LIFE,
WAS ALWAYS SENT TO A
FRIEND BY THE ANCIENT
ETRUSCANS WHEN THEY KNEW
THEY THEMSELVES FACED DEATH

IN MEMORY OF
EBENEZER TINNEY
WHO DIED MARCH 12, 1813
AGE 81 YEARS
MY GLASS IS RUM

EPITAPH in Grafton, Vt.

THE HUMAN MARIMBA
INDIAN MUSICIANS in early Guatemala
·PLAYED TUNES BY TAPPING GOURDS
*STRAPPED TO EACH MUSICIAN'S
WAIST*

MEMORIAL TO WORLD WAR I
in Bennwihr, Alsace, France,
WAS THE ONLY THING
UNHARMED BY AN AIR ATTACK
IN WORLD WAR II THAT
DESTROYED THE ENTIRE TOWN

LEATHERJACKET
THE FISH THAT CAN'T BE SCALED
ITS SCALES ARE SET AT
VARIOUS ANGLES

THE RAT-TRAP TREE
(Gliricidia sepium) of Venezuela
IS USED AS A LIVING
HEDGE BECAUSE ITS ROOTS
*ARE HIGHLY POISONOUS
TO RODENTS*

MARY LOU
and
**KAY SUE
VAN VOORHIS**
IDENTICAL
TWINS

WERE
MARRIED
TOGETHER
TO
LARRY JAY
AND GARY RAY
WAYBLE
*-ALSO
IDENTICAL
TWINS*

**KING
ZOUMAOU**
of the Mahi and Dassa
Tribes of Africa
UNABLE TO OWN A REAL
HORSE BECAUSE IT WOULD
BE KILLED BY TSETSE FLIES,
RODE THROUGH HIS KINGDOM
ON A WOODEN HORSE ON WHEELS

THE **MANSION** OF **DANGERFIELD** (England)

WAS LEASED FOR 71 YEARS WITH ITS ANNUAL RENTAL ONLY *THE FRAGRANCE OF ONE RED ROSE*

THE ROSE WAS PLACED ON A GATE POST ONCE EACH YEAR BY THE TENANT AND THE LANDLORD MERELY SMELLED ITS FRAGRANCE AS HE PASSED

TREE THAT FORMS A PERFECT "P"

JUDGE J.C. RUSSELL of Zapata County, Texas, SO ANNOYED THE DISTRICT ATTORNEY BY HIS HABIT OF SLEEPING ON THE BENCH THAT THE PROSECUTOR POURED HALF A POUND OF SUGAR INTO THE JURIST'S WATER PITCHER.

THE NEXT TIME THE JUDGE WASHED HIS FACE HIS BEARD BECAME CAKED WITH SUGAR - AND FLIES HARASSED HIM SO MUCH HE NEVER AGAIN FELL ASLEEP IN A COURTROOM

THE **MOSQUITO FERN** LOOKS LIKE A SWARM OF MOSQUITOES IN FLIGHT

LA MARTINIERE —in Lucknow, India, WAS BUILT BY GEN. CLAUDE MARTIN AS HIS HOME AND HE BEQUEATHED IT FOR USE AS A COLLEGE —BUT TO PREVENT THE LOCAL RULER FROM SEIZING IT AFTER THE GENERAL'S DEATH, MARTIN ORDERED *THAT HE BE BURIED IN ITS BASEMENT*

JADE COINS used in China FOR 1,300 YEARS *WERE SHAPED LIKE FISH*

Dr. Charles DELORME (1584-1678) celebrated French physician CONVINCED THAT WARM FEET WERE ESSENTIAL TO GOOD HEALTH **WORE 6 PAIRS OF NEW STOCKINGS TO BED EVERY NIGHT FOR 75 YEARS** HE NEVER WORE THE SAME STOCKINGS TWICE - DISCARDING 164,000 PAIRS AFTER USING THEM ONCE

CAPT. JOHN LOWER, JR. of Key West, Fla., WAS LICENSED AS A SHIP'S CAPTAIN *AT THE AGE OF 13*

SI MANCÒ
LA FORTVNA
NON IL VALORE
1°7·1942
← ALESSANDRIA

AN ITALIAN MONUMENT near El Alamein WHERE ITALY'S TROOPS WERE HALTED IN WORLD WAR II, BEARS THE INSCRIPTION: "We did not lack valor— we just ran out of luck"

18 CAMELS WERE REQUIRED TO CARRY TO THE CALIPH WALID THE BILLS FOR CONSTRUCTION OF the Omayyad Mosque of Damascus, Syria —TOTALING $29,000,000— *BECAUSE THE CALIPH REFUSED TO BELIEVE ANYONE COULD BE DISHONEST IN CONSTRUCTING A PLACE OF WORSHIP, HE PAID THE BILLS AND ORDERED THEM BURNED WITHOUT EXAMINATION* (709)

JAMES WRIOTHESLEY
(1605-1624) of Callington, England,
WAS ELECTED TO PARLIAMENT
AT THE AGE OF 15

A **TREE** GROWING THROUGH
THE ROOF OF A PORCH

KURAI
of Benares,
India,
A DEVOTEE
OF YOGI
PRAYED FOR
PERIODS OF
45 MINUTES
6 TIMES EACH
DAY FOR
27 YEARS
*WITH HIS
HEAD BURIED
IN THE
GROUND*

THE **ANGRY YOUNG MAN**
near Palm Springs, Calif.,
NATURAL STONE
FORMATION

THE VEILED WOMEN
of the Harasi Tribe, of Hadhramaut, Arabia,
MAY WEAR BLACK MASKS ONLY IF
THEIR REPUTATIONS ARE SPOTLESS

A **BARRISTER** in England
CANNOT
SUE
FOR
HIS
FEE

*IT IS
CONSIDERED
AN
HONORARIUM
—AND NOT
COLLECTIBLE
BY PROCESS
OF LAW*

MAX von HEES AT THE AGE OF 69 CLIMBED 9,200 FEET TO THE PEAK OF THE WILD EMPEROR MOUNTAIN IN AUSTRIA —HIS 1,500TH HAZARDOUS ASCENT

CASTEL del MONTE in Italy WAS BUILT WITH 8 OCTAGONAL TOWERS AND 8 HALLS AROUND AN OCTAGONAL COURT BY EMPEROR FREDERICK II OF GERMANY TO COMMEMORATE THE FACT THAT HE CAME OF AGE IN 1208

THE **STICK INSECT** of Borneo IS NATURE'S LARGEST INSECT —MEASURING 13 INCHES IN LENGTH

THE SHIP THAT WAS SAVED BY A BUBBLE!

THE "BOULE", A FRENCH BRIG, THE NAME OF WHICH MEANS "BUBBLE", CAPSIZED OFF THE SCILLY ISLES IN 1860, BUT IT WAS KEPT AFLOAT—AND 4 MEMBERS OF ITS CREW REMAINED ALIVE —*BECAUSE OF A HUGE BUBBLE OF AIR IN ITS SEALED HOLD*

THE EARL OF GALWAY

(1648-1720) a Frenchman who became an English general WAS CAPTURED BY THE FRENCH IN 1693, BUT HE HAD BECOME SO FAMED FOR HIS BRAVERY THAT HIS CAPTORS COULD NOT BRING THEMSELVES TO EXECUTE HIM FOR TREASON *SO THEY TURNED HIM FREE!*

ORGANPIPE CORAL

GROWS IN THE SHAPE OF CYLINDRICAL TUBES —*LIKE THE PIPES OF AN ORGAN*

HERE LIES
THE FORESTER ROBERT POTT
WHO DIED OF A RIFLE SHOT
HIS REAL NAME
WAS FRANZ LIME
BUT THAT WOULD NOT
HAVE BEEN IN RHYME

EPITAPH IN OBERALM CEMETERY
near Hallein, Austria

2 CLOUDS PHOTOGRAPHED
over Marseilles, France
*BOTH SHAPED LIKE
INVERTED FLYING SAUCERS*
Nov. 4, 1954

THE HORSESHOE CRAB
IS NOT A CRAB —
IT IS A SPIDER

THESE WOMEN REALLY RULE THE ROOST!
A WIFE
in the KHASSI Tribe, India,
CAN SEND HER HUSBAND
BACK TO HIS MOTHER
WITH A SNAP
OF HER FINGERS!

*IN HER DISMISSAL GESTURE
THE WIFE ALWAYS TOSSES
HER DISCARDED HUSBAND
5 COWRIE SHELLS AS ALIMONY*

FENCES AROUND MANY HOMES in Ameland, The Netherlands, *ARE MADE OF THE RIBS AND LOWER JAWS OF WHALES*

MICHEL MUSSON WHO INTRODUCED REGISTERED MAIL IN THE U.S., SPURNED THE JOB OF POSTMASTER GENERAL IN 1849 *PREFERRING TO SERVE AS POSTMASTER OF NEW ORLEANS, LA.*

HENRIETTA FRAME of Tucson, Ariz., HAS SCORED 3 HOLE-IN-ONES – ALL 3 IN GOLF GAMES PLAYED OVER A PERIOD OF 5 YEARS **ON MARCH 20th**

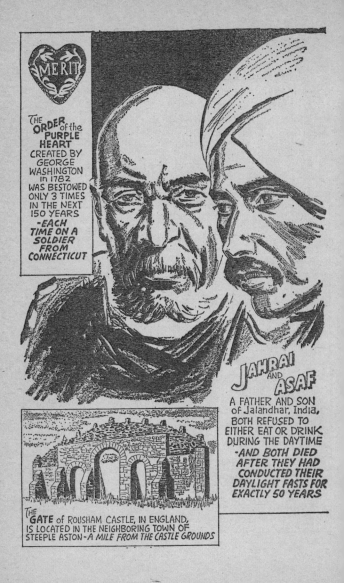

THE **ORDER** of the **PURPLE HEART** CREATED BY GEORGE WASHINGTON In 1782 WAS BESTOWED ONLY 3 TIMES IN THE NEXT 150 YEARS -EACH TIME ON A SOLDIER FROM CONNECTICUT

JAHRAI AND **ASAF** A FATHER AND SON of Jalandhar, India, BOTH REFUSED TO EITHER EAT OR DRINK DURING THE DAYTIME -AND BOTH DIED AFTER THEY HAD CONDUCTED THEIR DAYLIGHT FASTS FOR EXACTLY 50 YEARS

THE **GATE** of ROUSHAM CASTLE, IN ENGLAND, IS LOCATED IN THE NEIGHBORING TOWN OF STEEPLE ASTON -A MILE FROM THE CASTLE GROUNDS

NATALIE von **HOYNINGEN** of Lechts, Estonia, WROTE HER WILL WHILE LYING IN BED, FELT HER OWN PULSE AND SAID, "DEATH IS 5 MINUTES AWAY"-AND DIED EXACTLY 5 MINUTES LATER

HENRY MAURER of Westminster, Calif., CELEBRATED HIS 75th BIRTHDAY BY PLAYING 75 HOLES OF GOLF -WALKING ALL THE WAY

THE TUSKS OF BOARS on the island of Achin, Indonesia, ARE OFTEN TRAINED BY THE NATIVES TO GROW IN THE FORM OF 2 COMPLETE CIRCLES

OPTICAL ILLUSION
LINES "A" AND "B" ARE
ACTUALLY PARALLEL

JOHN BOIS (1561-1644)
of Nettlestead, England, WHO LATER
BECAME ONE OF THE COMPILERS OF
THE KING JAMES VERSION OF THE
BIBLE, READ THE OLD TESTAMENT
IN ITS ORIGINAL HEBREW AT
THE AGE OF 5

THE
**PARADISE
FISH**
MUST SURFACE FOR AIR
OR IT WILL DROWN

A PEACE MEMORIAL
IN THE CITY HALL
of St. Paul, Minn.,
A STATUE OF AN INDIAN
36 FEET HIGH AND
WEIGHING 60 TONS
REVOLVES CONSTANTLY

NOEL NATIVIDAD NOEL
1635-1684
WAS BORN INTO A FAMILY NAMED CHRISTMAS, ON CHRISTMAS DAY, OF A MOTHER WHO WAS HERSELF BORN DURING THE SAME HOLIDAY.
HIS NAME MEANS CHRISTMAS, CHRISTMAS, CHRISTMAS

from an old print

MARGAT a French balloonist MADE A SUCCESSFUL ASCENT FROM THE TIVOLI GARDENS in Paris *SEATED ON HIS PET STAG* — 1817 —

EYELESS SHRIMP ARE CAUGHT IN THE DARD RIVER IN A DARK CAVE NEAR Baumes-les-Messieurs, France, IN THE BELIEF THAT EATING THEM IMPROVES THE DINER'S EYESIGHT

A **CALENDAR WHEEL** used by the ancient Aztecs of Mexico TRACED THE INTRICATE ORBITS OF THE EARTH AND MOON AND ACCURATELY FORECAST ECLIPSES

THE MAN WHOM INSOLENCE MADE RICH AND FAMOUS!

BECRI MUSTAPHA, of Istanbul, BY REFUSING TO STEP OUT OF THE PATH OF SULTAN MURAD IV SO PIQUED THE INTEREST OF THE COUNTRY'S RULER *THAT HE MADE MUSTAPHA HIS CHIEF COUNCILOR*—FOR THE NEXT 10 YEARS MUSTAPHA WAS THE MOST IMPORTANT COMMONER IN THE TURKISH EMPIRE

THE FIRST THERMOMETER
IT WAS CREATED IN FLORENCE, ITALY, 300 YEARS AGO

THE CLOCK in the Church of Tirley, England, WAS CONSTRUCTED BY JOHN CARTER ENTIRELY FROM BROKEN-DOWN FARM IMPLEMENTS

The CHURCH THAT WAS CHALLENGED TO A DUEL!

ST. JAMES' CHURCH - Shipton, England, AGREED TO FIGHT A DUEL **AND WON THE CONTEST!**

ST. JAMES' REPRESENTATIVE DEFEATED THE LORD OF WENLOCK (1533)

MAYOR HIRAM GILL of Seattle, Wash., WHO WAS ELECTED IN 1910, SUBSEQUENTLY BECAME THE FIRST OFFICEHOLDER IN THE U.S. *TO BE VOTED OUT OF OFFICE*

A **PHEASANT** CAN EXIST WITHOUT EATING FOR **AN ENTIRE MONTH**

THE SOUND "EE" IN CHINESE *HAS 193 DIFFERENT MEANINGS*

THE MONUMENT TO AN OX
Baldhua Hill, India
A BULLOCK WON A BET FOR ITS OWNER BY CLIMBING THE 900-FOOT HILL WITH A FULL LOAD —*AND THEN FELL DEAD ON THE SUMMIT*

AL CLARK of Montezuma, Kansas, IN A 100-YARD RACE *OUTRAN A HORSE*

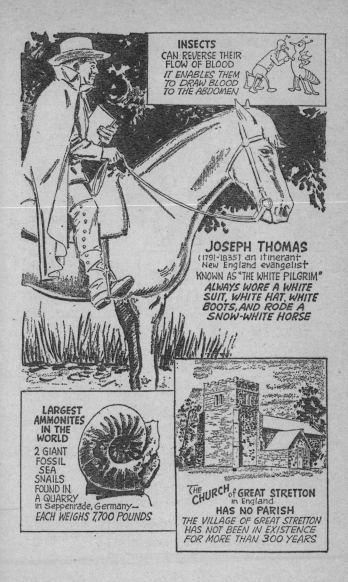

INSECTS
CAN REVERSE THEIR FLOW OF BLOOD
IT ENABLES THEM TO DRAW BLOOD TO THE ABDOMEN

JOSEPH THOMAS
(1791-1835) an itinerant New England evangelist
KNOWN AS "THE WHITE PILGRIM"
ALWAYS WORE A WHITE SUIT, WHITE HAT, WHITE BOOTS, AND RODE A SNOW-WHITE HORSE

LARGEST AMMONITES IN THE WORLD
2 GIANT FOSSIL SEA SNAILS FOUND IN A QUARRY
in Seppenrade, Germany—
EACH WEIGHS 7,700 POUNDS

The **CHURCH** of **GREAT STRETTON**
in England
HAS NO PARISH
THE VILLAGE OF GREAT STRETTON HAS NOT BEEN IN EXISTENCE FOR MORE THAN 300 YEARS

A **BRIDE** in the San Blas Tribe of Panama IS CONSIDERED LEGALLY MARRIED *IF SHE SITS FOR JUST A MINUTE IN THE YOUNG MAN'S HAMMOCK*

FEMALE BUTTON QUAILS of Africa FIGHT DUELS WITH EACH OTHER TO WIN THE ATTENTION OF THEIR CHOSEN MATES

THE **WINGED SNAIL** (Glaucus) HAS NO SHELL AND GROWS WINGS *WHICH ENABLE IT TO FLOAT ON THE WATER*

THE **PINKNEY BRIDGE**, England, CONSISTS ONLY OF STONES PILED WITHOUT MORTAR -*YET IT HAS ENDURED FOR CENTURIES*

JEFFERSON DAVIS PIERCE of Texarkana, Texas, WHO WAS NAMED FOR JEFF DAVIS, WAS BORN ON LINCOLN'S BIRTHDAY

KING KALUADEVA DEPOSED AS RULER OF Orissa. India, in 1542 WAS SENTENCED TO DIE BY BEING TRAMPLED BENEATH THE HOOVES OF THE HORSES IN A POLO GAME —SO NO ONE WOULD STAIN HIS HANDS WITH A KING'S BLOOD

THE OAK TREE in Giddings, Texas, FROM WHICH OUTLAW BILL LONGLEY WAS HANGED IN 1878 NEVER AGAIN SPROUTED NEW LEAVES

FRANCIS PHYLE (1720-1780) a Swiss soldier WHO HAD KILLED A MAN IN A DUEL, ATONED FOR WHAT HE CONSIDERED MURDER BY LIVING IN A CAVE OF THE BURR WOODS OF NEW JERSEY FOR 24 YEARS - WITHOUT EVER *BUILDING A FIRE FOR WARMTH OR MEALS*

KIRKBRIDE HOUSE in Mobile, Alabama, WHICH BECAME A LUXURIOUS RESIDENCE IN 1885, *WAS ORIGINALLY BUILT AS A JAIL - AND SERVED AS A PRISON FOR 168 YEARS*

MRS. FRANK LITTLE of River Falls, Wisc., WAS BORN, MARRIED AND DIED AT THE AGE OF 85 *IN THE SAME ROOM*

BACHELORS IN THE LANGO TRIBE, Africa, MUST LIVE IN HUTS SHAPED LIKE HAWKS

THE REV. JOHN SWEENEY (1834-1908) of Paris, Kentucky, WAS THE GRANDSON OF A MINISTER - THE SON OF A MINISTER -THE BROTHER OF 3 MINISTERS -THE FATHER OF 2 MINISTERS

THE "SUDBURY" AND "ISLAND SOVEREIGN" 2 DEEP-SEA TUGS, TOWED FOUR 3,000-TON TANKERS FROM BALBOA TO VICTORIA, B.C. -A DISTANCE OF 4,000 MILES (1954)

NERO'S DRINKING CUP WAS MADE OF MURRA —A FABULOUS LOST MATERIAL AND COST $360,000

CAMELS in the Canary Islands ARE EQUIPPED WITH RUMBLE SEATS AND TRANSPORT 2 RIDERS AND THEIR LUGGAGE

TURHAN wife of Sultan Ibrahim of Turkey, WAS THE MOTHER OF 3 TURKISH SULTANS —YET SHE HERSELF WAS A CHRISTIAN ALL HER LIFE.

Mrs. JOHN DURST
of Gillespie County, Texas,
WAS THE MOTHER OF 5 SONS
ALL NAMED JOHN

THE TEMPLES OF GOOD FORTUNE in Betul, India
EVERY FOREIGN OFFICER WHO HAS VISITED THE MUKTAGIRI TEMPLES
FOR THE LAST 200 YEARS *HAS RECEIVED AN IMMEDIATE PROMOTION IN RANK*

THE "HAIRY FROGS"
of the French Congo
HAVE HIPS AND THIGHS
COVERED WITH HAIR
*AN INCH
LONG*

THE CHURCH OF PORT ARTHUR
in Australia
WAS DESIGNED AND BUILT BY
JAMES BLACKBURN -A PRISONER
IN THE PORT ARTHUR JAIL—
*HE WAS GIVEN A FULL PARDON
UPON ITS COMPLETION IN 1840*

**BREAD
CAKE and
ROLLS**
are outlined
on the
wall of the
Cathedral
of Freiburg,
Germany,
SO PURCHASERS OF BAKERY PRODUCTS
CAN MAKE CERTAIN THEY HAVE
BEEN GIVEN FULL MEASURE

MONGOLIAN PRINCESSES
TRADITIONALLY FORBIDDEN
TO LEAVE HOME DURING THE
DAYTIME, ALWAYS WALKED
UNDER A CANOPY CARRIED
BY 2 ATTENDANTS
*- SO THEY WOULD BE STILL
UNDER THEIR PARENTAL ROOF*

SPINES of the Tuna Cactus of Argentina
ARE USED BY THE INDIANS
AS NEEDLES

THE MOST ROMANTIC CASTLE IN BELGIUM

THE PETITE SOMME CASTLE, NEAR LIEGE, WAS BUILT BY COUNT AMABLE de VAUX, WHOSE SWEETHEART AGREED TO MARRY HIM WHEN HE PROMISED THAT THEIR HOME WOULD DUPLICATE **THE MOST ROMANTIC CASTLE IN ALL OF FRANCE**

HE BUILT A REPLICA OF KING HENRI IV'S CASTLE AT PAU, FRANCE

A **GIRL** in rural areas of China WEARS A BRAID FOR EACH YEAR OF HER LIFE —WITH ONE EXTRA BRAID BECAUSE A CHINESE BABY IS CONSIDERED A YEAR OLD THE DAY SHE IS BORN

THE **LAFF** found in the Indian Ocean **IS THE MOST POISONOUS OF ALL FISH** —IT BURROWS INTO THE SAND, AND STEPPING ON THE HOLLOW SPINES OF ITS BACK BRINGS PAINFUL DEATH

THE NAIL VIOLIN
PLAYED BY GERMAN
MUSICIANS IN THE
18th CENTURY
*WAS A CIRCULAR
WOOD FRAME SPIKED
WITH 66 NAILS*
IT WAS PLAYED WITH
A CONVENTIONAL BOW

Emma
Foeltzer
BURNHAM
of Neenah, Wis.,
WAS SO
CIVIC MINDED
THAT WHEN G.A.
CUNNINGHAM
WROTE "THE
HISTORY
OF NEENAH,"
A BOOK OF
292 PAGES,
*SHE COPIED IT
IN LONGHAND
FOR FRIENDS
27 TIMES*

THE ROUND TOWER OF SIMIANE
THE ONLY STRUCTURE OF ITS KIND IN ALL FRANCE
HAS BAFFLED HISTORIANS FOR CENTURIES

HENRI MOUHOT
(1826-1861) A FRENCH TRAVELER IN INDOCHINA, IMPRESSED THE KING OF LUANG PRABANG SO FAVORABLY, THE MONARCH GAVE HIM AUTHORITY TO PARDON CRIMINALS AND *THE POWER OF LIFE AND DEATH OVER ALL THE KING'S SUBJECTS*

THE TEMPLE OF SAINTHIA
in India
WAS ERECTED TO HONOR
A STRIP OF BEDDING
THE RELIC WAS DISCARDED BY CHAITANYA—A RELIGIOUS LEADER— WHO SLEPT ON THE SITE OF THE TEMPLE IN 1800

THE **LARGEST AMPHIBIAN IN NATURE**
THE GIANT SALAMANDER of Japan
ATTAINS A LENGTH OF 5 FEET

DAVID R. CAMPBELL
(1794-1885) of Baltimore, Vt.,
SLEPT FOR 70 YEARS WITH
A LARGE STEEL THIMBLE
BENEATH HIS PILLOW
*IN THE BELIEF IT WOULD
PROTECT HIM FROM LIGHTNING*

THE **CATHEDRAL** of **AMIENS**
IS THE LARGEST IN ALL FRANCE

THE TURTLE
HAS NOT CHANGED IN
200,000,000 YEARS

THE REV. JOHN W. SUTTLE OF Cleveland County, N.C., WHO OFTEN SERVED 6 CHURCHES SIMULTANEOUSLY WAS A RURAL MINISTER FOR 65 YEARS

THE BOADICEA AN ENGLISH OYSTER SMACK WON A REGATTA IN HER CLASS ALTHOUGH SHE HAD BEEN IN CONSTANT SERVICE FOR 143 YEARS

THE ROYAL EXECUTIONER OF KING TIEBA OF Kenedugu, Africa, JUST PRIOR TO CUTTING OFF A VICTIM'S HEAD WAS REQUIRED TO PERFORM A DANCE TO ENTERTAIN HIM

A **GARDEN ARCH**
STILL STANDING IN
Newstead Abbey, England,
WAS ORIGINALLY THE
FRONT WALL OF AN ABBEY
-CONVERTED BY SIR JOHN
BYRON, AN ANCESTOR
OF THE POET BYRON,
424 YEARS AGO

A **CONFUCIAN
ROSARY**
FOUND IN THE
RUINS OF AN
ANCIENT TEMPLE
in the Gobi Desert

IS MADE OF
HUMAN BONES
STRUNG ON
GRASS

Patrick
MURRAY
(1703-1778)
SON OF THE 4th
EARL OF ELIBANK

WAS
COMMISSIONED
A CAPTAIN
IN THE
BRITISH
ARMY WITH
FULL PAY
-AT THE
AGE
OF 3
1706

JEAN-FRANCOIS CHAMPOLLION (1791-1832) FATHER OF EGYPTOLOGY AND THE FIRST TO SOLVE THE MYSTERY OF THE HIEROGLYPHICS, WAS PROFESSOR OF HISTORY at the University of Grenoble, in France — *AT THE AGE OF 17*

THE **MONASTERY** BUILT TO ATONE FOR A MURDER
Chamillé, France
KING HENRY II of England BUILT THIS MONASTERY IN 1178 IN THE BELIEF IT WILL EXPIATE THE MURDER OF THOMAS À BECKET *IF IT STANDS FOR 1,000 YEARS!*

THE **SAPUCAYA NUT** of Brazil GROWS IN A HARD SHELL, *SEALED WITH A TRIANGULAR "STOPPER"*— WHEN THE NUT RIPENS, THE "STOPPER" DROPS OUT

THE **MUDSKIPPER** BREATHES WHILE ON LAND *THROUGH THE TAIL WHICH IT KEEPS DIPPED IN THE WATER*

THE CORPSE of DAVID LIVINGSTONE (1813-1873) THE FAMED EXPLORER WHO DIED IN NORTHERN RHODESIA WAS CARRIED BY NATIVES *1,000 MILES THROUGH THE WILDERNESS WRAPPED IN A CYLINDER OF BARK — A TREK THAT TOOK 9 MONTHS!* HIS BODY WAS THEN SHIPPED HOME TO ENGLAND FOR BURIAL IN WESTMINSTER ABBEY

MONKEYS ARE TRAINED TO *HARVEST COCONUTS* in Padang, Indonesia

A *GIRL* in Rajasthan, India, TO MARK HER 13th BIRTHDAY DANCES IN A WHIRLING SKIRT *THE BOTTOM OF WHICH IS 13 YARDS IN CIRCUMFERENCE*

ABRAHAM BEAULIEU
ACCIDENTALLY SHOT
APRIL 4, 1844
AS A MARK OF AFFECTION
FROM HIS BROTHER

STRANGE EPITAPH
in the cemetery at LaPointe, Minn.

THE STREET OF THE 7 DEVILS in Jever, Germany, IS SO NAMED BECAUSE IN THE 18TH CENTURY 3 MEN AND 4 WOMEN LIVING ON IT WERE *EXECUTED FOR SORCERY*

ZELAD GOVERNOR OF A LARGE PART OF PERSIA AND ARABIA, WIPED OUT A CRIME WAVE IN HIS CITIES BY *THREATENING DEATH TO ANYONE ON THE STREET AFTER SUNDOWN—* TO EMPHASIZE HIS INTENTION TO CARRY OUT HIS EDICT HE ORDERED HIS PEOPLE TO *LEAVE EVERY DOOR UNLOCKED*

THE DEMON-FACED CRAB of Japan APPEARS TO BE WEARING A *GROTESQUE MASK*

HERE LIES THE BODY
OF WILLIAM HEWED
WHO DEPARTED THIS LIFE
NOVEMBER THE 19th 1718
AGED 218

EPITAPH
in Taddington, England

A **MAN** BRAVING THE COLD IN THE
ANTARCTIC WITH HIS FACE UNCOVERED
*IN A FEW SECONDS FINDS IT
ENCASED IN A MASK OF ICE*

THE **GATE** near Chambéry, France,
THROUGH WHICH THE ALPINE
HIGHWAY NOW PASSES, WAS
BUILT IN THE 15th CENTURY
AS THE ENTRANCE ARCH TO
THE CHURCH OF ST. DOMINIC
*WHICH WAS DEMOLISHED
200 YEARS AGO*

DOG TRICYCLE INVENTED BY
A FRENCHMAN NAMED GUITU
*THE WHEELS WERE REVOLVED
BY 2 RUNNING DOGS*

W ⑂ U. ⊙.

A REBUS USED IN THE U.S. 100 YEARS AGO TO DUN DEBTORS— *IT READS: FORK OVER W-HAT YOU OWE*

GEORGE WITHER (1588-1667) the English poet CAPTURED BY A ROYALIST BAND IN 1642 AND SENTENCED TO DEATH, WAS SAVED BY SIR JOHN DENHAM, A ROYALIST POET, ON THE PLEA THAT WHILE WITHER WAS ALIVE SIR JOHN DENHAM "COULD NOT BE CALLED ENGLAND'S WORST POET"—*WITHER NEVER FORGAVE SIR JOHN FOR THE ARGUMENT THAT SAVED HIS LIFE*

COURT OFFICIALS ARE SO IN AWE of the ruler of Jakarta, in Java, THAT WHEN PASSING THE THRONE ROOM THEY ALWAYS FALL TO THEIR KNEES, CRAWL TO THE THRESHOLD, AND RAISE THEIR HANDS IN PRAYER TO THE MARBLE THRONE —*EVEN WHEN THE ROOM IS EMPTY*

DONKEYS BEARING WATER IN THE ANDES MOUNTAINS of South America ARE BLINDFOLDED —*BECAUSE* THEY MIGHT BALK IF THEY WERE ALLOWED TO SEE HOW LARGE A LOAD THEY CARRY

THE GRAVESTONES THAT MARK NO GRAVES

THE MARINE CEMETERY of Narbonne, France, CONTAINS ONLY MEMORIALS TO NATIVE FISHERMEN AND SAILORS *WHOSE BODIES HAVE NEVER BEEN FOUND*

DANIEL McCARTHY (1641-1752) of County Kerry, Ireland, MARRIED HIS 5th WIFE —A GIRL 14 YEARS OF AGE— WHEN HE WAS 84— HE LIVED ANOTHER 27 YEARS —AND THEY HAD *20 CHILDREN*

THE **AXOLOTL** IS A REPTILE
THAT NEVER GROWS UP —
IT LIVES OUT ITS ENTIRE
LIFETIME AS THE LARVAL FORM
OF THE TIGER SALAMANDER

A **CHURCH**
in Bühl,
Germany,
WAS MADE THE
CITY HALL
*IN THE BELIEF
THAT NO
POLITICIAN
WOULD BE
DISHONEST
IN SO HOLY
A STRUCTURE*

SULTAN SULEYMAN
(652-702) of Khorasan
ORDERED BY HIS SUPERIOR TO
SURRENDER FOR EXECUTION
GENERAL YEZID, WHOSE SAFETY
HE HAD GUARANTEED,
*CHAINED HIMSELF TO THE
PRISONER AND VOWED THEY
WOULD DIE TOGETHER* —
THE CALIPH RESCINDED HIS
ORDER AND LIBERATED BOTH MEN

PYGMY FISHERMEN of the Congo River, THEIR BODIES CAMOUFLAGED BY FOLIAGE, REMAIN SUBMERGED AT THE BOTTOM OF THE RIVER *UNTIL THEIR NET IS FILLED WITH FISH*

THE **ELIZABETH GATE** In Heidelberg, Germany, *WAS CONSTRUCTED IN A SINGLE NIGHT IN 1620 BY PRINCE FREDERICK V AS A BIRTHDAY SURPRISE FOR HIS WIFE ELIZABETH— IT HAS ENDURED FOR 344 YEARS*

DR. ROBERT SOUTHGATE (1741-1833) of Scarborough, Me., WHO GAVE UP HIS MEDICAL PRACTICE TO BECOME AN ATTORNEY WAS A JUSTICE OF THE PEACE FOR 40 YEARS -YET NOT A SINGLE VERDICT HE RENDERED WAS EVER APPEALED TO A HIGHER COURT

THE **TOMBS**
of the Kings of the Bunyoro Tribe
of Africa
COMMAND THE GREATEST
REVERENCE -YET -THEY
**CONTAIN ONLY THE
MONARCHS' JAWBONES**—
*THE REST OF EACH DEAD
KING'S BODY IS ALWAYS
INTERRED IN AN
UNMARKED GRAVE*

**SHEIK
MUHAMMAD
bin ISA**
of Kajgaon, India,
SAT WITH HIS EYES TIGHTLY
SHUT FOR 12 YEARS
*TO ATONE FOR TURNING HIS
BACK UPON A MOSQUE
FOR A SINGLE INSTANT*

THE
**STONE
MAN**

NATURAL
ROCK
FORMATION
in Bonifacio,
Corsica

THE HUMAN BRIDGES

JAPANESE TROOPS INVADING MALAYA IN WORLD WAR II CROSSED SWAMPS AND SHALLOW BODIES OF WATER ON BRIDGES CONSISTING OF LOGS *SUPPORTED ON THE SHOULDERS OF SPECIALLY TRAINED ENGINEERS*

THE **EMPEROR'S CLOCK**

A CLOCK BOAT 2½ FEET LONG MADE FOR RUDOLPH II of Germany IN 1580— *THE FIGURES MOVE AROUND THE DIAL AND MARK THE HOURS BY BOWING TO A MINIATURE THRONE*

NATIVES of Paillin, Cambodia, SIFT MUD IN THE BED OF THEIR SHALLOW RIVER FOR *PRECIOUS RUBIES AND SAPPHIRES*

THE DEADMAN BROTHERS ARE FUNERAL DIRECTORS in Manchester, Tenn.

THE 40-PENNY ROAD between Mantes and St. Germain, France, GETS ITS NAME FROM THE FACT THAT ITS BUILDER WAS FORCED BY A LABOR SHORTAGE IN 1780 TO PAY THE FABULOUSLY HIGH WAGE OF 40 CENTS A DAY

The HANGING GARDENS of BRAZIL LARGE LUMPS OF EARTH PLACED IN THE FORKS OF TREES BY ANTS —WHICH SOW SEEDS IN THEM AND THEN CULTIVATE THE PLANTS

LORENZO CELSI a Venetian Admiral WAS ELECTED DOGE - OR RULER - OF VENICE BY SPREADING THE FALSE RUMOR THAT HE HAD DEFEATED AN ARMADA OF PIRATES— HIS DECEIT WAS DISCOVERED AFTER HIS ELECTION - BUT HE WAS PERMITTED TO RETAIN HIS POST

THE STALAGMITE STATUE
Cave of Bossea, Italy
IT WAS NAMED "JOSEPHINE" BY
ITS DISCOVERER BECAUSE IT WAS
*A REMARKABLE LIKENESS
OF HIS OWN WIFE*

AN
ANCIENT
HEATHEN
ALTAR
at Saint Remy,
France,
HAS EARS
SCULPTURED
ON IT SO
WORSHIPERS
COULD
*WHISPER
DIRECTLY
INTO THE EARS
OF THE ROMAN
GODDESS
BONA DEA*

AVRIBVS

CALIPH YEZID II
(683-724) of Damascus
BECAUSE HIS MOST BEAUTIFUL
SLAVE CHOKED TO DEATH ON
A RAISIN HE TOSSED INTO
HER MOUTH, LITERALLY
DIED OF A BROKEN HEART—
*THE DOCTOR PRONOUNCED THE
CAUSE OF THE CALIPH'S DEATH
AS A RIFT IN HIS HEART*

THE COLLEGIATE CHURCH OF OUR LADY OF LOCHES
France
WAS BUILT WITHOUT A SINGLE HORIZONTAL LINE

ITS BRICK WALLS AND SPIRES WERE ERECTED UNEVENLY AS A WHIM OF ITS DONOR

THE CAP CACTI

A CACTUS in Peru THAT SEEMS TO BE *WEARING A TURKISH CAP*

ROBERT SOUTHEY (1774-1843)

THE FAMED ENGLISH POET, WAS REFUSED PERMISSION TO LEASE A HOUSE IN Resolven, Wales, *BECAUSE THE LANDLORD FELT A POET COULD NOT AFFORD THE RENT OF $25 A YEAR*

NATURE'S GUN MOUNT

THE **GREAT GUN** of Murshidabad, India
17½ FEET LONG — WEIGHING **7** TONS —
WAS RAISED 4 FEET OFF THE GROUND
BY THE ROOTS OF A PEEPUL TREE

**MIDWIFE
TOAD**
(Alytes
obstetricans)
WHICH HATCHES
ITS YOUNG BY
WINDING A STRING
OF EGGS AROUND
ITS HIND LEGS
IS A MALE

CHARLES de VOLVIRE
(1630 - 1692)
of Bois de la Roche Castle, France,
WAS THE FATHER OF
**ST. ANNE TOUSSAINT,
A PRIEST, AND 7 NUNS**

THE BUTTERFLY BOATS OF AFRICA

THE FISHING VESSELS of the Kotokos of the Chari River HAVE WINGS FASHIONED FROM FISHING NETS —*IN THE BELIEF IT GIVES THEM GREATER SPEED*— .THE BOATS ARE MADE OF WOODEN PLANKS —SEWN TOGETHER WITH VEGETABLE VINES

MAURICE ADOLPHE LINANT (1799-1883)

WHO BECAME CHIEF ENGINEER FOR THE SUEZ CANAL WAS CHIEF HYDRAULIC ENGINEER OF ALL EGYPT *AT THE AGE OF 16*

BOVINE OSCAR

THE CHAMPION MILK PRODUCER IN EACH SWISS HERD WEARS AS A CROWN *A MILKING-STOOL FIRMLY ROPED ON ITS HEAD*

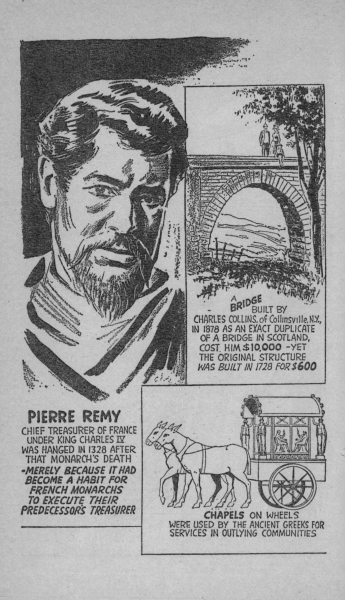

A **BRIDGE** BUILT BY CHARLES COLLINS, of Collinsville, N.Y., IN 1878 AS AN EXACT DUPLICATE OF A BRIDGE IN SCOTLAND, COST HIM $10,000 —YET THE ORIGINAL STRUCTURE WAS BUILT IN 1728 FOR $600

PIERRE REMY
CHIEF TREASURER OF FRANCE UNDER KING CHARLES IV WAS HANGED IN 1328 AFTER THAT MONARCH'S DEATH —MERELY BECAUSE IT HAD BECOME A HABIT FOR FRENCH MONARCHS TO EXECUTE THEIR PREDECESSOR'S TREASURER

CHAPELS ON WHEELS WERE USED BY THE ANCIENT GREEKS FOR SERVICES IN OUTLYING COMMUNITIES

A TRIUMPHAL ARCH in Fano, Italy, BUILT IN 10 B.C. IN HONOR OF ROMAN EMPEROR AUGUSTUS *WAS CONVERTED INTO THE ENTRANCE TO THE CHURCH OF FANO 1,521 YEARS LATER—* IT IS STILL IN USE

HUSSEIN MEZZO MORTO A BARBARY PIRATE WHO BECAME RULER OF ALGIERS ADOPTED THE NAME "MEZZO MORTO" BECAUSE HE WAS CRITICALLY WOUNDED IN A BATTLE WITH THE SPANIARDS —*THE NAME MEANING "HALF DEAD"*

THE SHELL of the Hemicardium Oyster IS SHAPED LIKE A *HEART*

THE **TOWER** of the CHURCH of St. LAMBERT in Munster, Germany, STILL FEATURES 3 CAGES CONSTRUCTED TO EXHIBIT *THE HEADS OF 3 CRIMINALS EXECUTED IN 1536*

THE CRAYFISH HAS TEETH IN ITS STOMACH AND *ITS LIVER IN ITS HEAD*

KING ANDRAS II who ruled Hungary from 1205 to 1235 SAT IN JUDGMENT ON AN ASSASSIN WHO HAD KILLED THE MONARCH'S WIFE – AND DECLARED IT A JUSTIFIABLE MURDER! *4 YEARS LATER, THE KING, LEAVING ON A CRUSADE, APPOINTED THE QUEEN'S KILLER REGENT OF HUNGARY*

WILLIAM BILLINGE
WAS BORN IN A CORNFIELD
in Longnor, England,
*AND DIED 112 YEARS LATER
IN THE SAME CORNFIELD*

THE HOUSES IN THE TOWN OF GHAT
in the Sahara Desert
ARE ALL BUILT WITHOUT ROOFS

THE "BUSINESS CARD"
SENT BY
RAY SIMPSON of Delta, Colo., TO
DESPERADOES WHO THREATENED
REVENGE BECAUSE HE HAD
FOILED A BANK HOLDUP, WAS
A SQUARE OF BLACK CARDBOARD,
PERFORATED BY 10 BULLET
HOLES FORMING A TIGHT CIRCLE
*FIRED BY SIMPSON FROM
A DISTANCE OF 225 FEET*

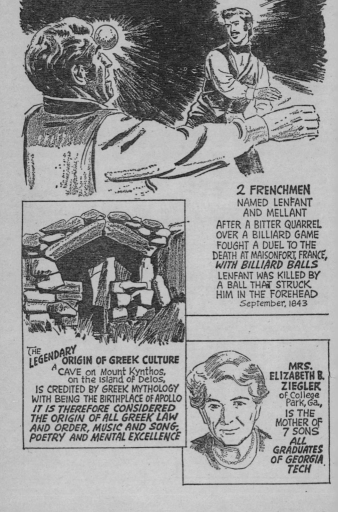

2 FRENCHMEN NAMED LENFANT AND MELLANT AFTER A BITTER QUARREL OVER A BILLIARD GAME FOUGHT A DUEL TO THE DEATH AT MAISONFORT, FRANCE, *WITH BILLIARD BALLS* LENFANT WAS KILLED BY A BALL THAT STRUCK HIM IN THE FOREHEAD September, 1843

THE **LEGENDARY ORIGIN OF GREEK CULTURE** A CAVE on Mount Kynthos, on the Island of Delos, IS CREDITED BY GREEK MYTHOLOGY WITH BEING THE BIRTHPLACE OF APOLLO *IT IS THEREFORE CONSIDERED THE ORIGIN OF ALL GREEK LAW AND ORDER, MUSIC AND SONG, POETRY AND MENTAL EXCELLENCE*

MRS. ELIZABETH B. ZIEGLER of College Park, Ga., IS THE MOTHER OF 7 SONS *ALL GRADUATES OF GEORGIA TECH*

THESE SYMBOLS REPRESENT THE NUMBER 3252¾ OOO\\ ooo))vv
–AND THEY WERE USED BY THE ANCIENT CRETANS *4,000 YEARS AGO* – THE CRETANS USED SYMBOLS REPRESENTING DIGITS FROM ONE TO 10–AND EVEN FRACTIONS

THE CITY NO TRAVELER HAS ENTERED WITH EMPTY HANDS

ADRAR, LOCATED IN MAURITANIA IN THE SAHARA DESERT, HAS 60 WELLS –EACH 60 FEET DEEP– AND NO VISITOR HAS BEEN PERMITTED TO ENTER THE CITY FOR 3,000 YEARS UNLESS HE BEARS WITH HIM *A ROPE 150 FEET LONG WITH WHICH TO DRAW WATER*

JOHN LINCOLN KEHOE III
of New York City
WAS BORN ON *FEBRUARY 12.*
HIS FATHER,
JOHN LINCOLN KEHOE, JR., WAS BORN *FEBRUARY 12.*
HIS GRANDFATHER,
JOHN LINCOLN KEHOE, SR., WAS BORN *FEBRUARY 12.*
–3 *SUCCESSIVE GENERATIONS BORN ON LINCOLN'S BIRTHDAY*

THE GHOST VILLAGE OF VANNO
the Eolian Islands, Italy,
ABANDONED BY ALL ITS INHABITANTS
TWICE IN THE PAST 100 YEARS—
*EACH TIME ITS RESIDENTS
EMIGRATED TO AMERICA*

**THE MAN WHOSE HAIR TURNED
WHITE IN HOURS**
Jean Baptiste Brizard
(1721-1791) the famed French actor
SAVED HIMSELF WHEN A
SHIP SANK IN THE RIVER
RHONE BY CLINGING TO
AN IRON RING BENEATH A
BRIDGE FOR 11 HOURS—
*BRIZARD WAS ONLY 30 YEARS
OF AGE, BUT HIS BLACK
HAIR TURNED SNOW WHITE
BEFORE HE WAS RESCUED*

**A POCKET
KNIFE**
SHAPED LIKE
A LADY'S SHOE
*GIVEN TO SUITORS BY FRENCH
LADIES OF THE 18th CENTURY
—MEANT THEY WERE BEING
GIVEN "THE BOOT"*

QUEEN ISABELLA de ANGOULEME of England AFTER THE DEATH OF HER HUSBAND, KING JOHN, MARRIED HUGH de LUSIGNAN *THE FIANCÉ OF HER OWN DAUGHTER, JOANNA* 1220

MOURNERS at Chinese funerals WIELD HUGE BROOMS *TO CLEAR THE DECEASED'S PATH OF EVIL SPIRITS*

PRAYER FLAGS ARE FLOWN IN MONGOLIA AND IT IS BELIEVED A PRAYER HAS BEEN UTTERED EACH TIME *THE BANNER FLUTTERS IN THE WIND*

A **WHALE** HARPOONED OFF THE COAST OF AUSTRALIA, WAS LANDED ON THE WHALER "JOHN and WINTHROP" *ONLY AFTER IT HAD BITTEN IN HALF 2 WHALEBOATS* (1886)

A **PIECE** *of CLOTH* KEPT IN THE Imperial Treasury in Vienna, Austria, AS PART OF THE REGALIA USED BY EMPERORS AT THEIR CORONATIONS, *WAS ORIGINALLY PART OF THE TABLECLOTH AT THE LAST SUPPER*

POLICE JUDGE **FRANK H. LOWE** of Glendale, Calif., NEVER STUDIED LAW—YET *NO DECISION HE MADE WAS EVER REVERSED BY A HIGHER COURT IN 28 YEARS OF SERVICE ON THE BENCH*

MR. and MRS. JOHN J. ZAVISHLOCK

CELEBRATED THEIR 50th WEDDING ANNIVERSARY AT A PARTY ATTENDED BY 6 OF THEIR CHILDREN -*EACH OF WHOM WAS ALSO CELEBRATING HIS OR HER OWN WEDDING ANNIVERSARY* (Oct. 21, 1963)

THE EGG CHURCH
In Mgart, on the island of Malta, IS SO CALLED BECAUSE ITS CONSTRUCTION WAS FINANCED SOLELY BY CONTRIBUTIONS OF *ONE OF EVERY 10 EGGS LAID BY HENS IN THE AREA*

NATIVES
of New Guinea *HAVE "POCKETS" ON THEIR ARMS* THEY CARRY THEIR KNIVES, MONEY AND OTHER SMALL ARTICLES BENEATH THONGS WRAPPED AROUND THEIR BICEPS

THE **ENGAGEMENT** "RING"
GIVEN TO GIRLS OF the Bhutia Tribe of the Himalayas IS A SHELL WHICH THE BRIDE-TO-BE WEARS *AS A BRACELET*

THE DEVIL'S SLIDE
In Weber Canyon, Utah,
A NATURAL STONE FORMATION
300 FEET LONG
WITH ROCK WALLS
20 FEET APART

Alfred
VAIL
(1807-1859) of Morristown, N.J.
INVENTED THE
ALPHABET OF
DOTS AND DASHES
KNOWN AS THE
MORSE CODE

THE BRIMSTONE BUTTERFLY
HIBERNATES THROUGH THE ENTIRE WINTER
CLINGING TO THE TWIG OF A HOLLY BUSH
—WITH NO PROTECTION FROM
THE BITTER COLD

GENERAL WILLIAM MACKINTOSH
(1662-1743) A SCOTTISH JACOBITE, OFFERED HIS FREEDOM IF HE WOULD ADMIT THE SOVEREIGNTY OF KING GEORGE I – *REFUSED AND SPENT THE REMAINING 24 YEARS OF HIS LIFE IN A PRISON CELL IN EDINBURGH CASTLE*

CHARLES GREEN
of London, England,
MADE AN HOUR-LONG FLIGHT IN A BALLOON, SEATED ON *THE BACK OF A PONY*
(July 29, 1828)

THE *HALF DIME* MINTED IN 1792 *WAS THE FIRST U.S. COIN*

CHAIN SPOONS USED BY THE Barotse Tribe of Rhodesia —WITH BOTH SPOONS AND THEIR CONNECTING CHAIN CARVED FROM *A SINGLE BLOCK OF WOOD*

MRS. NICHOLAS COMEAU of Lewiston, Me., WAS THE MOTHER OF 11 SONS —*ALL NAMED JOSEPH*— AND 4 DAUGHTERS —*ALL NAMED MARIE*

A LARGE BUILDING in Chelsea, Mich., WAS PAINTED BY 100 MEN IN 1959 *IN 3 MINUTES, 9 SECONDS*

KUDU COWS in Africa ARE OFTEN ACCOMPANIED BY TICKBIRDS – *WHICH WARN THEM OF APPROACHING DANGER IN RETURN FOR A CONTINUOUS FEAST OF PARASITES*

POTATO CHIP SHAPED LIKE A TREBLE CLEF

GIROLAMO CARDANO
(1501 - 1576)
FAMED ITALIAN MATHEMATICIAN BECAUSE ONE SON HAD BEEN EXECUTED FOR MURDER WAS GIVEN PERMISSION BY COMPASSIONATE AUTHORITIES TO DECIDE THE **PUNISHMENT TO BE METED OUT TO HIS DELINQUENT OTHER SON**– *THE FATHER ORDERED THAT HIS SECOND SON'S EARS BE CUT OFF*

THE HOUSE THAT CAME FROM A PACK OF CARDS

BELLVUE MANSION in Edinburgh, Scotland, WAS BUILT FOR GEN. JOHN SCOTT BY SIR LAURENCE DUNDAS *WHEN HE LOST A CARD GAME*

ARTHUR de BOISSIEU
(1835-1873) famed French writer
WAS SO SUPERSTITIOUS THAT AT
THE AGE OF 38 - A FEW HOURS
BEFORE HE WAS TO HAVE BEEN THE
13th GUEST AT A DINNER PARTY—
HE DIED OF FRIGHT (March 29, 1873)

THE
WINDMILL of **RYE**
England
IS NOW USED
AS A GARAGE
*YET IT MUST BE
MAINTAINED AS A
WINDMILL BY
ITS LESSEE
FOREVER*

THE **JOHN
DORY**
TRAILS
HAIRLIKE
FINS
*AS LONG AS
ITS ENTIRE
BODY*

THE
CLITOCYBE MUSHROOM
GLOWS WITH A BLUE
HUE IN THE DARKNESS
-AND IS WARM TO
THE TOUCH

THE FIRST FATAL AUTOMOBILE ACCIDENT IN HISTORY

A STEAM AUTOMOBILE INVENTED IN Paisley, Scotland, BY SCOTT RUSSELL, EXPLODED ON A REGULAR RUN FROM GLASGOW TO PAISLEY ON JULY 29, 1834 *KILLING ALL 5 OCCUPANTS*

THE **TOMBSTONE** of an ancient Roman tool manufacturer *ADVERTISED HIS ENTIRE LINE OF PRODUCTS*

WHITE PIGEON a Potawatomi Indian chief, TO WARN SETTLERS IN WHITE PIGEON, MICH., OF AN IMPENDING INDIAN ATTACK, RAN ALL THE WAY FROM DETROIT - A DISTANCE OF 150 MILES - HE SAVED THE SETTLEMENT, BUT COLLAPSED AND DIED (1830)

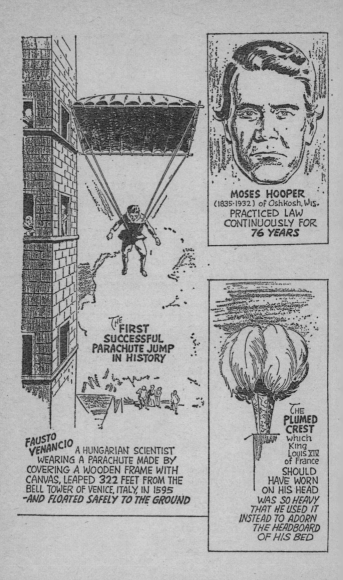

MOSES HOOPER
(1835-1932) of Oshkosh, Wis.
PRACTICED LAW
CONTINUOUSLY FOR
76 YEARS

THE
**FIRST
SUCCESSFUL
PARACHUTE JUMP
IN HISTORY**

**FAUSTO
VENANCIO** A HUNGARIAN SCIENTIST
WEARING A PARACHUTE MADE BY
COVERING A WOODEN FRAME WITH
CANVAS, LEAPED **322 FEET** FROM THE
BELL TOWER OF VENICE, ITALY, IN 1595
-AND FLOATED SAFELY TO THE GROUND

THE **PLUMED
CREST**
which
King
Louis XIV
of France
SHOULD
HAVE WORN
ON HIS HEAD
WAS SO HEAVY
THAT HE USED IT
INSTEAD TO ADORN
THE HEADBOARD
OF HIS BED

A **TIN TUB**

SERVES ON THE EUPHRATES RIVER, in Syria,
AS AN EXCURSION BOAT

The **WHIRLIGIG BEETLE**

TO ESCAPE ITS SURFACE ENEMIES CRASH DIVES UNDERWATER WITH
A BUBBLE OF AIR TRAPPED BENEATH ITS WING COVERS

WILLIAM MARSHAL
(1670-1792) of London, England,
MARRIED 17 TIMES
AND EACH OF HIS BRIDES WAS
EXACTLY 26 YEARS OF AGE
-YET HE SURVIVED ALL OF THEM EXCEPT THE LAST ONE

THE **SAVOY PALACE**
in London, England,
WHICH HAS BEEN DESCRIBED AS THE
MOST BEAUTIFUL MANSION IN EUROPE
*WAS LEASED TO PETER OF SAVOY
BY KING HENRY III IN 1246*
**FOR AN ANNUAL RENTAL
OF 3 BARBED ARROWS**

THE **BASQUES** of
France
and Spain

IN A DANCE
CALLED THE
TXANKARRENKO
**MUST
WHIRL
AND HOP
FOR A
FULL HOUR
ON ONE LEG**

-IF A
DANCER
LOWERS THE
OTHER LEG
HE MUST
START
OVER

THE **GILT ROOM** of **HOLLAND HOUSE**
London, England, HAS NOT BEEN
RE-DECORATED SINCE IT WAS
PREPARED FOR THE MARRIAGE OF
KING CHARLES 1 AND QUEEN MARIA
HENRIETTA **339 YEARS AGO**

Sir Edwyn SANDYS (1561-1629) WAS A MEMBER OF THE ENGLISH PARLIAMENT AND THE ANCESTOR OF 7 GENERATIONS, IN EACH OF WHICH THE ELDEST SON WAS ELECTED TO PARLIAMENT— IT REPRESENTED A CONSECUTIVE LINE OF 211 YEARS

3 WOODEN CHAIRS WERE THE ONLY FURNITURE OWNED BY BETSY WHITLOCK of Brandon, Vt., AND EXCEPT WHEN SHE WAS ENTERTAINING SPECIAL COMPANY SHE HUNG THE CHAIRS ON WALL HOOKS TO PROTECT THEM FROM WEAR

THE **DOME OF THE ROCK** in Jerusalem WAS COVERED WITH 3,392 SHIELDS OF SOLID GOLD BY THE 2 ARCHITECTS WHO DESIGNED THE MOSQUE —A DONATION OF THEIR ENTIRE FEE OF SOME $600,000 (685-691)

JOHANN MICHAEL WIDMAN
(1642-1736)
OFFICIAL EXECUTIONER OF Nuremberg, Germany,
PERSONALLY CUT OFF EVERY VICTIM'S HEAD OVER A *PERIOD OF 70 YEARS*

MONEDA STREET in Cuenca, Spain,
IS AT THE BOTTOM OF A DEEP CANYON SO NARROW THAT OCCUPANTS OF HOUSES OVERHANGING THE CLIFFS *CAN SHAKE HANDS ACROSS THE STREET*

To my Blubber

VALENTINES 150 YEARS AGO in New England WERE LETTERED IN GILT ON THE HIDE OF A WHALE

AN **OPENING** NEAR THE ENTRANCE TO A CAVE IN Port Arthur, Tasmania, IS AN ALMOST-PERFECT OUTLINE OF THE MAP OF TASMANIA

ABDALAHI SHEIKH SYDIA
CHIEF OF A RELIGIOUS BROTHERHOOD IN Mauritania, Africa, WAS BORN ON THE BACK OF A CAMEL —AND FOR THE FIRST 10 YEARS OF HIS LIFE NEVER TASTED A DROP OF WATER

THE **BED** ON WHICH PRINCE EUGENE OF SAVOY (1663-1736) LAY IN STATE AFTER HIS DEATH HAS BEEN PRESERVED UNCHANGED **FOR 228 YEARS**

SANTA MARIA A VILLAGE IN THE CANTON OF GRISONS, Switzerland **IS IN THE SHAPE OF A PERFECT CROSS**

GILBERT ANTOINE de ST. MAXENT LIEUTENANT GOVERNOR OF FLORIDA AND LOUISIANA **WAS THE FATHER OF A GOVERNOR OF FLORIDA AND THE FATHER-IN-LAW OF 2 GOVERNORS OF LOUISIANA**

THE OLDEST PAINTING OF A EUROPEAN A PAINTING OF A PRINCE FOUND ON THE WALLS OF the Palace of Knossos, Crete, **WAS CREATED MORE THAN 4,000 YEARS AGO**

THE IMPERIAL MUSHROOM
IT IS SO CALLED BECAUSE IN THE DAYS OF THE ROMAN EMPIRE IT COULD ONLY BE SERVED IN THE PALACE OF THE EMPEROR - AND A COMMONER WAS FORBIDDEN EVEN TO TOUCH IT

THE ANCHOR INN in Sidlesham, England, WAS LEASED TO DIONES GEERE IN 1609 FOR AN ANNUAL RENTAL OF 8 PENCE *THE EQUIVALENT OF 16 CENTS* - THE LEASE TO RUN FOR 1,000 YEARS

EL CID *Spains greatest hero* **WAS ALSO ITS FIRST BULLFIGHTER** *EL CID KILLED A BULL IN AN ARENA WITH A LANCE IN 1040*

THE **SITE** OF THE **ENTIRE VILLAGE** of St. Annes, Lancashire, England, WAS LEASED BY ITS OWNER TO A COMPANY IN 1875 *FOR A PERIOD OF 1,100 YEARS*

Christopher **COLUMBUS** WAS THE "MOST BORN" AND THE "MOST BURIED" MAN IN HISTORY!

30 CITIES CLAIM HIS NATIVITY— HE HAS BEEN GIVEN 26 DIFFERENT YEARS OF BIRTH— HE WAS BURIED 8 TIMES

THE **CHAPEAU ISLANDS,** Taranaki, N.Z. TINY ISLANDS THAT LOOK LIKE LADIES' FLOPPY HATS *—EVEN TO THE BRIM BINDINGS AROUND THE BASE OF THE CROWN*

THE **ROCKAWAY VALLEY RAILROAD** WHICH RAN ITS FIRST TRAIN IN NEW JERSEY IN 1888 SO STARTLED RESIDENTS OF THE AREA THAT ROBERT THOMPSON, AN 80-YEAR-OLD FARMER, **DIED OF SHOCK**

THE **TORPEDO SNAIL** A MARINE MOLLUSK of Bermuda **LOOKS LIKE A MINIATURE TORPEDO**

POTATO MARTIAN

SUBHANA, THE WORST A NAME BESTOWED IN JEST BY AN ENGLISH CUSTOMER ON A SHAWL MERCHANT in Srinagar, Kashmir, SO PLEASED HIM THAT HE ADOPTED IT AS **THE OFFICIAL TITLE OF HIS BUSINESS**

THE **MEDIEVAL GATE** of Schladming, Austria, WAS STARTED IN 1630 —BUT WASN'T COMPLETED TILL **300 YEARS LATER**

FROGS of the Eleutherodactylus group ARE NEVER TADPOLES —HATCHING AS PERFECTLY FORMED FROGS

JUDGES in the Dan Tribe of Liberia ARE FORBIDDEN TO HAND DOWN DECISIONS *UNLESS THEY ARE MASKED.*

MANCHESTER, VT., **42** BIRTHS
IN 1963 **42** MARRIAGES
RECORDED **42** DEATHS

THE **CUPOLA** of the MOSQUE of HON
BUILT IN 1840 IN THE OASIS OF
Gioffra, Libya,
IS A COPY OF A SAILOR'S HAT

OSCAR
MARTIN **CARTER**
(1842-1928)
THE FOUNDER OF
HOUSTON, Texas,
SERVED SIMULTANEOUSLY
AS PRESIDENT OF
7 DIFFERENT BANKS

THE **FISH THAT HAS HEADLIGHTS**
(Photoblepharon)
BANDA ISLANDERS of Indonesia
USE THE LUMINOUS ORGAN
OF THIS FISH AS BAIT
*BECAUSE IT CONTINUES TO
SHINE EVEN AFTER ITS
REMOVAL FROM THE FISH*

A **SINGLE FARMHOUSE** COMPRISES THE *ENTIRE PARISH OF BOWERDALE,* England

Calf BORN WITH **2 NOSES 3 EYES** and **6 LEGS**

LOUISE BURNS (1840-1910) of Salem, Ohio, A FORTUNE TELLER ENJOINED FROM PRACTICING MEDICINE WITHOUT A LICENSE, TOOK THE STATE MEDICAL EXAMINATION WITHOUT PREPARATION *-AND PASSED IT SHE SERVED AS A LICENSED PHYSICIAN FOR 40 YEARS*

THE GRAVESTONE
of a philanthropist buried
near Tuggurt, Algeria,
HAS OPENINGS INTO WHICH HIS
RELATIVES DROP COINS FOR THE
POOR – *SO THE DEAD MAN CAN
MAINTAIN HIS REPUTATION*
EVEN AFTER DEATH

**LAMINARIA
DIGITATA**
an alga of the
North Sea

HAS A STEM
SHAPED LIKE
A CORKSCREW

**ELDERLY
KOREAN
MEN**

WEAR BLACK
HATS TO SHOW
THEY ARE
MARRIED AND
SWITCH TO
WHITE HATS
TO ANNOUNCE
THEY ARE
**WIDOWERS
SEEKING A
NEW WIFE**

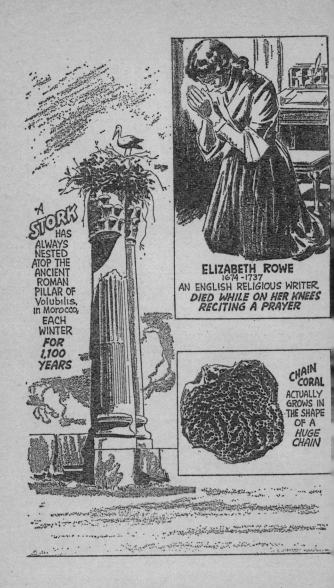

A STORK HAS ALWAYS NESTED ATOP THE ANCIENT ROMAN PILLAR OF Volubilis, in Morocco, EACH WINTER FOR 1,100 YEARS

ELIZABETH ROWE
1674-1737
AN ENGLISH RELIGIOUS WRITER
DIED WHILE ON HER KNEES RECITING A PRAYER

CHAIN CORAL ACTUALLY GROWS IN THE SHAPE OF A *HUGE CHAIN*

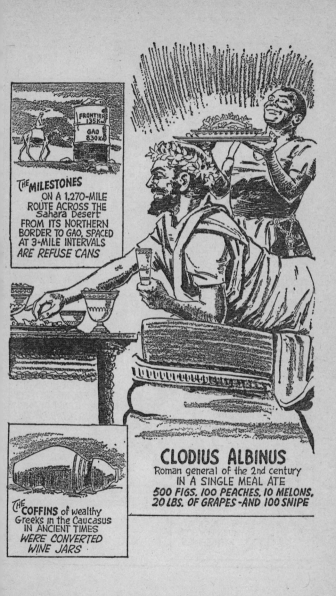

THE MILESTONES ON A 1,270-MILE ROUTE ACROSS THE Sahara Desert FROM ITS NORTHERN BORDER TO GAO, SPACED AT 3-MILE INTERVALS *ARE REFUSE CANS*

THE COFFINS of wealthy Greeks in the Caucasus IN ANCIENT TIMES *WERE CONVERTED WINE JARS*

CLODIUS ALBINUS
Roman general of the 2nd century
IN A SINGLE MEAL ATE
500 FIGS, 100 PEACHES, 10 MELONS, 20 LBS. OF GRAPES—AND 100 SNIPE

JANOSIK NOTORIOUS ROBIN HOOD of Slovakia SENT TO THE GALLOWS IN 1713, WAS GRANTED AS HIS FINAL REQUEST, AN ORCHESTRAL ACCOMPANIMENT SO HE COULD *GAILY FOLK DANCE FOR AN HOUR BEFORE THE TRAP WAS SPRUNG*

THE **CHURCH TOWER** in Stoney Middleton, England, WAS BUILT BY JOAN EYRE IN GRATITUDE FOR THE SAFE RETURN OF HER HUSBAND FROM THE BATTLE OF AGINCOURT IN 1415 —AND ALTHOUGH THE ADJOINING CHURCH HAD TO BE REBUILT *THE ORIGINAL TOWER STILL STANDS AFTER 549 YEARS*

THE **THORNY OYSTER** (Spondylus Regius) IT IS COVERED WITH SPINES

THE MURDER INN
of Berlin, Germany,
WAS GIVEN THAT NAME AS
A WHIM BY ITS FOUNDER
-YET IN LESS THAN A YEAR
THE OWNER AND HIS
ENTIRE FAMILY WERE
MURDERED (1837)

GLOVES USED
BY CRIMINALS
IN EUROPE
HAVE
RUBBERIZED
FINGERTIPS.

ON
WHICH
THE
FINGER-
PRINTS
OF A DEAD
MAN HAVE
BEEN ETCHED

**THE LUCKIEST GIRLS
IN THE WORLD!**
A GIRL of the LENGUA TRIBE
of Bolivia
CAN CHOOSE AS HER
HUSBAND ANY BACHELOR
IN THE TRIBE -AND
HE CAN'T SAY NO!

THE **CATERPILLAR** OF THE Congolese Moth CAMOUFLAGES ITS SILK NEST BY COVERING IT WITH SCORES OF SMALL STICKS

LION GARDINER
(1599-1641)

WAS THE FIRST ENGLISH SETTLER IN THE STATE OF NEW YORK

HIS DAUGHTER ELIZABETH WAS THE FIRST ENGLISH CHILD BORN IN NEW YORK

AND HIS SON DAVID WAS THE FIRST WHITE CHILD BORN IN CONNECTICUT

THE **CATHEDRAL** OF FREDERICTON in New Brunswick, Canada, IS AN EXACT REPRODUCTION OF THE CHURCH OF ST. MARY in Snettisham, England

THE FIRST DIRIGIBLE

3 CIGAR-SHAPED BALLOONS LASHED TOGETHER AND FILLED WITH HYDROGEN GAS BY AN AMERICAN INVENTOR NAMED DR. SOLOMON ANDREWS PROVED COMPLETELY MANEUVERABLE AND COVERED 30 MILES IN 14½ MINUTES -IN 1863

PIERRE ALAIN
of Arras, France, GAVE EACH OF HIS TRIPLET SONS THE FIRST NAME OF PÈRE -FRENCH FOR "FATHER" ALL 3 BECAME PÈRE PÈRE -BECAUSE ALL 3 BECAME PRIESTS

MARSTON ALEXANDER AGE 13 and **LAYNE NEWMAN** AGE 9

IN THE SAME ROUND OF GOLF AT THE DALLAS C.C. Texas

BOTH SCORED A HOLE IN ONE

CARLO ANTONIO DELPINI (1740-1828)

FAMED ENGLISH-ITALIAN CLOWN WHO WAS TERRIFIED OF THE NUMBER "8" ALL HIS LIFE, DIED IN 1828 AT THE AGE OF 88!

RINGS WERE LEGAL TENDER IN Ireland IN THE 12th CENTURY

THE TIGERS THAT DRINK SALT WATER
Sundarbans, India
THEY QUENCH THEIR THIRST WITH SEAWATER FROM TIDAL RIVERS WITH NO APPARENT HARM

THE PETROLEUM FLY LARVA
(Helaeomyia petroli)
WHICH BREATHES THROUGH A TINY SNORKEL, *THRIVES IN POOLS OF PETROLEUM*

WALTER J. DICKINSON
(1832-1899)
WHO BECAME HISTORIAN
of Randolph, Ohio,
READ THE BIBLE FROM COVER TO COVER AT THE AGE OF 7

THE MAN WHO LEAPED ACROSS THE CUYAHOGA RIVER
CAPT. SAM BRADY
(1756-1795)
FAMED PENNSYLVANIA COLONIST AND HERO OF THE REVOLUTION,
TO ESCAPE PURSUING INDIANS AT Kent, Ohio, IN 1780
MADE A 27-FOOT JUMP OVER THE CUYAHOGA RIVER

A TUMBLER
BEING WASHED BY Mrs. JANICE ALAGNA
CRACKED TO FORM A PERFECT LETTER "A"
Cicero, Ill.

MRS. VIRGINIA LEAVY
of Greensburg, Pa.,
HAD AN OPEN SAFETY PIN REMOVED FROM HER LUNG
-WHERE IT HAD BEEN EMBEDDED FOR 14 YEARS

A RACCOON WAS TRAINED BY OWEN JONES, OF STEUBEN HILLS, N.Y., TO EAT AT ITS OWNER'S TABLE, DRINK COFFEE, AND *DUNK BREAD IN COFFEE, SOUP OR LIQUOR*

ZEIN EDDIN ALI (523-563) GOVERNED THE PROVINCES OF SINJAR, HARRAN AND ARBELA, IN Iraq, EFFICIENTLY FROM 558 TO 563 *—YET HE WAS TOTALLY DEAF AND BLIND*

LA MALAGA (1772-1852) CELEBRATED PARISIAN ROPE WALKER LOST ALL HER TEETH AT THE AGE OF 60 *—BUT GREW AN ENTIRELY NEW SET AT THE AGE OF 79*

THE *NEST* OF THE MUD DAUBER *RESEMBLES A MUSICAL INSTRUMENT KNOWN AS THE PIPES OF PAN*

A **12-MILE SCENIC HIGHWAY** from Girvan to Ballantrae, Scotland, WAS ESTIMATED BY FAMED ENGINEER THOMAS TELFORD TO COST $75,000 -YET A LAYMAN BUILT THE ROAD TO TELFORD'S SPECIFICATIONS FOR $25,000 -AND MADE A PROFIT OF $5,000 (1804)

FARMERS in Haiti OFTEN WALK TO MARKET *WITH LARGE ROUND BREADFRUITS BALANCED ON THEIR HEADS*

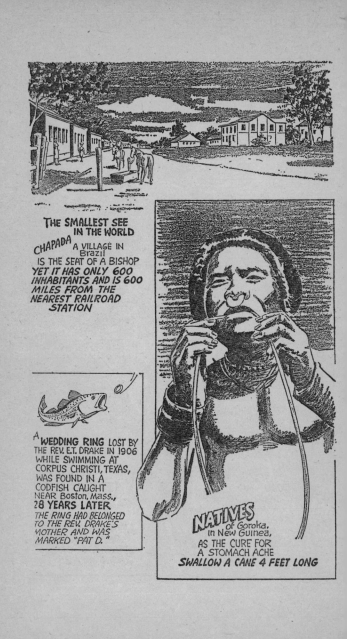

THE SMALLEST SEE IN THE WORLD

CHAPADA A VILLAGE IN Brazil
IS THE SEAT OF A BISHOP
YET IT HAS ONLY 600
INHABITANTS AND IS 600
MILES FROM THE
NEAREST RAILROAD
STATION

A WEDDING RING LOST BY
THE REV. E.T. DRAKE IN 1906
WHILE SWIMMING AT
CORPUS CHRISTI, TEXAS,
WAS FOUND IN A
CODFISH CAUGHT
NEAR Boston, Mass.,
28 YEARS LATER
THE RING HAD BELONGED
TO THE REV. DRAKE'S
MOTHER AND WAS
MARKED "PAT D."

NATIVES of Goroka,
in New Guinea,
AS THE CURE FOR
A STOMACH ACHE
SWALLOW A CANE 4 FEET LONG

BEGGARS in Algeria KEEP A HAND EXTENDED FOR ALMS *EVEN WHEN THEY ARE ASLEEP*

HOMES of the IRAPA PYGMIES of Venezuela CAN BE CONSTRUCTED *IN JUST A FEW MINUTES*

THE SHORT-TAILED SHREW IS THE ONLY MAMMAL *WITH A POISONOUS BITE*

THE TEMPLE BUILT TO COMMEMORATE ONE HONEST ACT

GAURI SEN of Boralpara, India, ORDERED 7 SHIPLOADS OF ZINC SENT TO A CUSTOMER —BUT BY ERROR THE VESSELS WERE LOADED WITH SILVER. *The customer revealed the mistake and Sen built the Temple of Siva with the money he saved*

SCALA PRETIOSA A TYPE OF WENTLETRAP SHELL *LOOKS LIKE A PILE OF DISHES*

WOMEN in Peru WERE FORBIDDEN TO LOAF BY THEIR ANCIENT INCA RULERS —SO CENTURIES LATER *THEY STILL KNIT AS THEY WALK ABOUT THE STREETS*

THE MECHANICAL HORSE
A TRICYCLE INVENTED by Gaetano Brianza in Milano, Italy, in 1819, THAT WAS OPERATED BY LEVERS WHICH *THE DRIVER PULLED WITH BOTH HANDS*

THIS IS THE **NEW YEAR—**
155,521,972,849,034
in India
IT IS THE 27th GRANDAGE OF THE 7th PATRIARCHATE OF BRAHMA'S LIFE—
THE ENTIRE LIFE OF BRAHMA TO DATE IS EQUAL TO BUT ONE WINK OF HIS EYE

HYPODERMA DIANA A European fly, *HAS A FACE LIKE A MONKEY*

"MOUNTAIN TIME" 4 PEAKS OVERLOOKING SESTO, in the Italian Dolomites, ARE NAMED "NINE," "ELEVEN," "TWELVE" AND "ONE," AND PEASANTS WORKING IN THE FIELDS CAN TELL THE TIME BECAUSE THE SUN IS ALWAYS OVER EACH MOUNTAIN PEAK EXACTLY *AT THE HOUR OF ITS NAME*

TOBA INDIANS of Bolivia AS A PROTECTION AGAINST NIGHTMARES *WEAR NIGHT AND DAY LONG CHAINS MADE OF FISH SCALES*

THE LIGHT-HEADED LOCUST of Brazil ITS ALLIGATOR-SHAPED HEAD *SHINES BRIGHTLY AT NIGHT*

THE **BRIDGE** of **BARK**

A BRIDGE CROSSING A RIVER BETWEEN AGADIR and IMMOUZER, Morocco, *CONSISTS OF A SINGLE PIECE OF BARK STRIPPED FROM A GIANT TREE*

SULTAN **MOHAMMED VI**

(1891-1929)

MOUNTED THE THRONE OF TURKEY AFTER HAVING BEEN A PRISONER FOR **57 YEARS**

HE HAD BEEN PLACED UNDER STRICT HOUSE ARREST WHEN HE WAS AN INFANT ONLY **4 MONTHS OF AGE**

TEXAS!

?

"TEXAS" IN THE LANGUAGE OF THE CENIDE INDIANS MEANS *"WE ARE PALS"*

WITHERSHAM WINDMILL in England
ITS SWEEPS MADE NON-OPERATIVE,
*NOW SERVES AS A
BRITISH ADMIRAL'S HOME*

THE HONEY GUIDE
an African bird
LEADS TRAVELERS TO THE
NESTS OF WILD BEES
*BECAUSE AFTER MEN HAVE
COLLECTED THE HONEY
THE BIRD WILL HAVE
ACCESS TO ITS OWN
FAVORITE REPAST
-THE YOUNG
BEES*

CHARLES CROS
(1842-1898) of Paris, France,
CELEBRATED POET
AND INVENTOR,
WAS SO PRECOCIOUS
A LINGUIST THAT HE
TUTORED 2 COLLEGE
PROFESSORS IN
HEBREW AND SANSKRIT
*WHEN HE WAS
11 YEARS OF AGE*

A COUPLE in the Watusi Tribe of Rwanda, Africa, ARE MARRIED WHEN EACH TAKES A MOUTHFUL OF WATER *AND SQUIRTS THE OTHER*

THE **MAN WHO HAD A VOICE LIKE A FOGHORN** ANDERSON GRAY HAD A VOICE SO POWERFUL THAT WHILE ADDRESSING MEETINGS ON THE ISLAND OF KINNAKEET, N.C., HE COULD BE DISTINCTLY HEARD OVER THE POUNDING OF THE SURF AT A POINT *2 MILES AWAY!*

2 HORSES HAULED FROM THE MICHIGAN PINEWOODS TO THE ONTONAGON RIVER, A LOAD OF LUMBER MEASURING 36,055 BOARD FT. — WHICH ROSE TO A HEIGHT OF 33.3 FT. AND WEIGHED 144 TONS — *THE LOAD MADE THE FINAL STAGE OF ITS JOURNEY ON 9 FLATCARS*

THE FLOATING VILLAGE OF CAMBODIA
SNOC TROU, A COMMUNITY IN WHICH ALL THE HOUSES *FLOAT ON THE SURFACE OF A LAKE*

ZULU MOTHERS WEAR THEIR HAIR IN SUCH A MANNER THAT THEIR CHILDREN -RIDING PIGGY-BACK- *CAN CLING TO IT*

THE STRANGEST MILITARY DEFENSE IN MODERN HISTORY
THE DESIGN OF AN ANCIENT LUCKY COIN WAS TRACED IN THE SANDS OF BEACHES BY THE JAPANESE IN WORLD WAR II *IN THE BELIEF IT WOULD WARD OFF AMERICAN BOMBERS*

A **HOUSE** in Glasgow, Scotland, THAT IS NOW USED AS A RESTAURANT WAS CONSTRUCTED IN 1872 *ENTIRELY OF CAST IRON*

THE **SAW-WHET OWL** IS SO NAMED BECAUSE ITS HOOT *SOUNDS LIKE THE HONING OF A SAW*

R. MASON JACKSON of Steubenville, Ohio, A CLERK IN THE AMERICAN CONSULATE IN Stuttgart, Germany, FOR STOPPING BOYS FROM THROWING SNOWBALLS AT A PASSING STRANGER WAS MADE A BARON OF THE KINGDOM OF WÜRTTEMBERG— *THE MAN HE ASSISTED PROVED TO BE KING KARL I OF WÜRTTEMBERG* (1873)

SPECIALLY BUILT TRAILERS FOLLOW THE KING OF SAUDI ARABIA ON HIS TRAVELS ACROSS THE DESERT *TO TRANSPORT HIS HAREM*

CALF WITH 6 LEGS

THE GREATEST GLUTTON OF THEM ALL!

THE 1st DUKE of BOLTON (1630-1698) FOR THE FINAL 25 YEARS OF HIS LIFE, SAT DOWN TO DINNER EACH NIGHT AT 7 P.M. AND DID NOT ARISE FROM THE TABLE UNTIL 8 A.M. THE NEXT DAY - *13 HOURS LATER*

THE CORKSCREW COLUMNS of the Hotel d'Alphonce, in Pezañas, France, WERE INSPIRED BY THE LONG CURLS OF THE BUILDER'S 16-YEAR-OLD DAUGHTER

A **HIPPOPOTAMUS** MADE OF BLUE GLAZED POTTERY WAS FOUND IN AN ANCIENT EGYPTIAN TOMB – HAVING BEEN PUT THERE 4,000 YEARS AGO *SO THE SOUL OF THE INTERRED HUNTER COULD ENJOY HIS FAVORITE SPORT AFTER DEATH*

MARY HARTEAU FIRST SCHOOL TEACHER of Morgan, Wis., WAS SO FEARFUL OF WEARING OUT HER SHOES, THAT SHE WALKED THE 6 MILES TO AND FROM SCHOOL EACH DAY *BAREFOOTED*

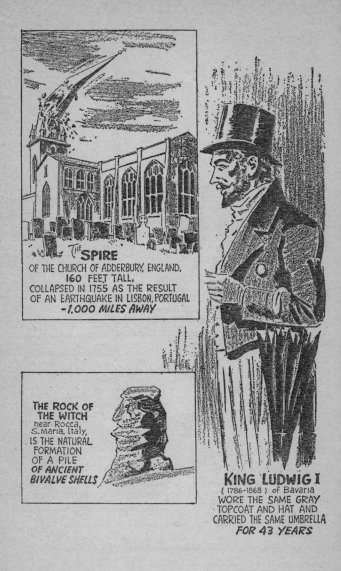

THE **SPIRE**
OF THE CHURCH OF ADDERBURY, ENGLAND,
160 FEET TALL,
COLLAPSED IN 1755 AS THE RESULT
OF AN EARTHQUAKE IN LISBON, PORTUGAL
-1,000 MILES AWAY

THE ROCK OF
THE WITCH
near Rocca,
S. Maria, Italy,
IS THE NATURAL
FORMATION
OF A PILE
OF *ANCIENT*
BIVALVE SHELLS

KING LUDWIG I
(1786-1868) of Bavaria
WORE THE SAME GRAY
TOPCOAT AND HAT AND
CARRIED THE SAME UMBRELLA
FOR 43 YEARS

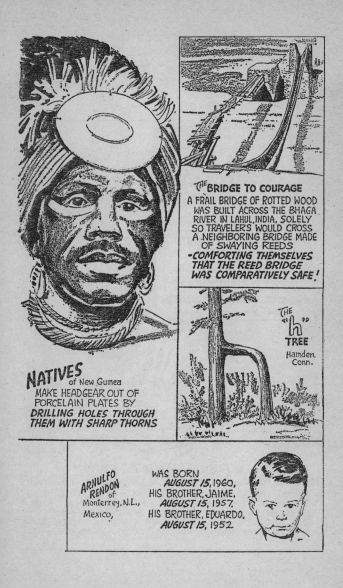

THE BRIDGE TO COURAGE
A FRAIL BRIDGE OF ROTTED WOOD WAS BUILT ACROSS THE BHAGA RIVER IN LAHUL, INDIA, SOLELY SO TRAVELERS WOULD CROSS A NEIGHBORING BRIDGE MADE OF SWAYING REEDS —*COMFORTING THEMSELVES THAT THE REED BRIDGE WAS COMPARATIVELY SAFE!*

THE **"h" TREE**
Hamden, Conn.

NATIVES of New Guinea MAKE HEADGEAR OUT OF PORCELAIN PLATES BY *DRILLING HOLES THROUGH THEM WITH SHARP THORNS*

ARNULFO RENDON of Monterrey, N.L., Mexico, WAS BORN *AUGUST 15*, 1960, HIS BROTHER, JAIME, *AUGUST 15, 1957*, HIS BROTHER, EDUARDO, *AUGUST 15, 1952*

THE OLDEST GLOVE IN THE WORLD
IT WAS FOUND IN KING TUT'S TOMB -AND IS MORE THAN 3,300 YEARS OLD

THE LAKE THAT WAS CREATED BY A SINGLE RAIN!

LAKE ALACHUA near Gainesville, Fla., 12 MILES LONG - APPEARED SUDDENLY ON A PRAIRIE AFTER A STORM AND VANISHED AGAIN 18 YEARS LATER!

THE BUSIEST MAN IN ALL HISTORY

PLINY, THE ELDER (23-79) WAS GOVERNOR of Germany, Gaul, Spain and Africa, A GENERAL AND ADMIRAL IN THE ARMED FORCES OF ANCIENT ROME, AND AT THE SAME TIME WROTE A NATURAL ENCYCLOPEDIA IN 37 VOLUMES, A HISTORY OF ROME IN 31 VOLUMES, A HISTORY OF ROMAN WARFARE IN 20 VOLUMES, A MANUAL OF ORATORY IN 6 VOLUMES, AND AN 8-VOLUME LATIN GRAMMAR

A **CABIN** BUILT OF ROCKS near Las Vegas, Nev., IN 1869 WAS WRECKED BY A STORM THAT SAME YEAR - AND THE ROCKS WERE FOUND TO CONTAIN ORE WORTH $75,000

J.O. PARRISH of Claremont, Calif., MADE A HOLE-IN-ONE -USING A GOLF CLUB HE FORGED HIMSELF FROM THE AXLE OF AN OLD CAR

RIZA HASAN (1809-1859) A YOUNG GROCERY CLERK IN ISTANBUL, TURKEY, BECAME GENERAL OF ALL THE TURKISH ARMIES AND GRAND ADMIRAL OF TURKEY'S FLEET -*BECAUSE HE WAS COURTEOUS TO A CUSTOMER IN HIS GROCERY-* THE CUSTOMER PROVED TO BE SULTAN MAHMOUD II -TRAVELING INCOGNITO

MAJOR THOMAS BIDDLE of St. Louis, Mo., and SPENCE PETTIS, A CANDIDATE FOR CONGRESS, BECAUSE BIDDLE WAS NEAR-SIGHTED, FOUGHT A GUN DUEL AT A DISTANCE OF *ONLY 5 FEET* BOTH MEN WERE KILLED (Aug. 27, 1831)

THE JAPANESE WALNUT GROWS IN THE SHAPE OF A PERFECT HEART

A TEAM OF ELK TRAINED BY JOHN DUNBAR of Swan City, Nebr. *TO PULL A WAGON* (1868)

KNIVES USED BY THE MAORIS of New Zealand *HAVE SHARKS' TEETH AS THEIR CUTTING EDGE*

THE **ROUGHEST COURTSHIP IN HISTORY**
Hector McNeill of Harnett County, N.C.,
TO WIN THE HAND OF SUSANNAH BARKSDALE
HAD TO FIGHT HER FATHER 3 TIMES
IN THE THIRD BATTLE HECTOR LOST AN EYE
AND BARKSDALE'S NOSE WAS BITTEN OFF
—BUT THE COUPLE MARRIED AND BECAME
THE PARENTS OF 9 CHILDREN (1780)

THE CEREMONIAL DRESS of the JIVAROS of Ecuador IS MADE OF BIRD BONES, MONKEY TEETH AND BEETLE WINGS

THE PORCH OF TRIUMPH
of the Church of St. Jacob,
in Koesfeld, Germany,
ORNATE EXAMPLE OF
12TH-CENTURY ARCHITECTURE
**WAS SHATTERED INTO THOUSANDS
OF FRAGMENTS BY WORLD WAR II**
BOMBS — *AFTER THE WAR
IT WAS RESTORED EXACTLY
-FROM THE ORIGINAL FRAGMENTS*

THE **WORST COUNTERFEITING
JOB IN HISTORY**
A CONFEDERATE BILL
REPRESENTING ITSELF ON
ONE SIDE AS WORTH $20
-AND ON THE OTHER
$1,000

EMPEROR KAO TSU II
of China
SURVIVED COUNTLESS ENEMY
ATTACKS IN BATTLE, ONLY TO
DIE IN A PAROXYSM OF RAGE
OVER AN INSULT FROM
KING LEAO OF THE TARTARS
CONTAINED IN A LETTER (992)

GENERAL PIERRE DAUMESNIL (1777-1832) WHO HAD A LEG BLOWN OFF BY A SHELL WHILE SERVING UNDER NAPOLEON IN THE BATTLE OF WAGRAM, COMFORTED HIS GRIEVING ORDERLY BY JESTING: *"WHAT ARE YOU WEEPING ABOUT? NOW YOU WILL HAVE ONLY ONE BOOT TO SHINE EACH MORNING!"* (1809)

THE **TOWER** of St. Philip's Church, in Charleston, S.C., SERVED FOR YEARS AS A LIGHTHOUSE, *ITS FIXED WHITE LIGHT BEING VISIBLE 18 MILES AT SEA*

"BLACKIE" A FIREHOUSE DOG IN BROOKLYN *SAVED A CAT FROM A BURNING BUILDING IN 1936 BY CARRYING IT DOWN A LADDER*

THE **BRONZE STATUE** of NIKLAUS von FLUE (1417-1487) THE RENOWNED SWISS STATESMAN, in the Church of Sachseln, Switzerland, **CONTAINS HIS BONES**

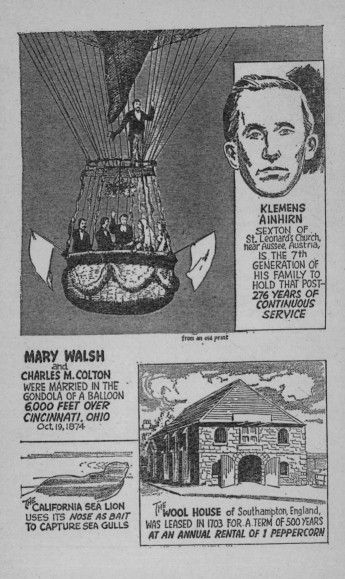

from an old print

KLEMENS AINHIRN SEXTON OF St. Leonard's Church, near Aussee, Austria, IS THE 7th GENERATION OF HIS FAMILY TO HOLD THAT POST—*276 YEARS OF CONTINUOUS SERVICE*

MARY WALSH and **CHARLES M. COLTON** WERE MARRIED IN THE GONDOLA OF A BALLOON *6,000 FEET OVER CINCINNATI, OHIO* Oct. 19, 1874

THE **CALIFORNIA SEA LION** USES ITS *NOSE AS BAIT* TO CAPTURE SEA GULLS

THE **WOOL HOUSE** of Southampton, England, WAS LEASED IN 1703 FOR A TERM OF 500 YEARS *AT AN ANNUAL RENTAL OF 1 PEPPERCORN*

THE NEEDLE FISH HAS JADE-GREEN BONES

LOPE de VEGA
(1562-1635)
SPANISH POET AND PLAYWRIGHT
WROTE 4,100 BOOKS AND PLAYS

THE TOMB THAT PROTECTED A SPIRIT FROM TEMPTATION
A NATIVE WOMAN of Lai Chau, Vietnam, WAS BURIED AT HER OWN REQUEST IN A LOW STRAW-COVERED GRAVE —WITH ALL HER COSMETICS PLACED ON A TALL BAMBOO STRUCTURE SO THEY WOULD BE BEYOND HER REACH

THE **MARBLE STATUE** OF **HENRY CLAY** in Louisville, Ky., *HAD TO BE CARVED TWICE* — THE FIRST STATUE WAS LOST IN A SHIPWRECK WHILE BEING TRANSPORTED FROM FLORENCE, ITALY

PAUL SCARRON, THE ELDER, FATHER OF THE FRENCH POET OF THE SAME NAME *NEVER WAS WITHOUT A COPY of the Epistles of St. Paul* WHICH HE READ AT EVERY OPPORTUNITY *FOR A PERIOD OF MORE THAN 30 YEARS*

THE MOST ROMANTIC MEMORIAL IN THE U.S.A. THE CHURCH OF THE WILDERNESS near Ligonier, Pa., A REPLICA OF THE TOMB OF RACHEL IN THE HOLY LAND, WAS BUILT BY JAMES ROSS MELLON IN 1925 IN LOVING MEMORY OF HIS WIFE — *WHO WAS NAMED RACHEL*

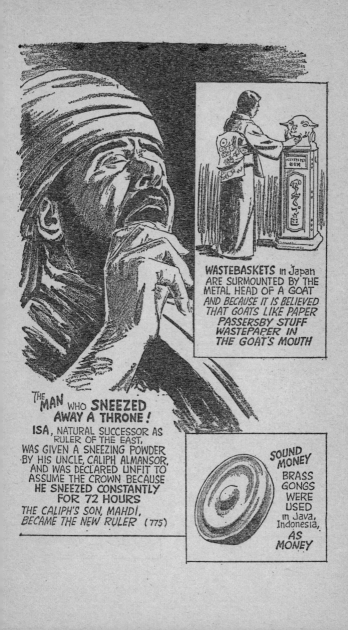

WASTEBASKETS in Japan ARE SURMOUNTED BY THE METAL HEAD OF A GOAT *AND BECAUSE IT IS BELIEVED THAT GOATS LIKE PAPER PASSERSBY STUFF WASTEPAPER IN THE GOAT'S MOUTH*

THE MAN WHO SNEEZED AWAY A THRONE!

ISA, NATURAL SUCCESSOR AS RULER OF THE EAST, WAS GIVEN A SNEEZING POWDER BY HIS UNCLE, CALIPH ALMANSOR, AND WAS DECLARED UNFIT TO ASSUME THE CROWN BECAUSE **HE SNEEZED CONSTANTLY FOR 72 HOURS** *THE CALIPH'S SON, MAHDÍ, BECAME THE NEW RULER* (775)

SOUND MONEY BRASS GONGS WERE USED in Java, Indonesia, AS MONEY

CHI CHANG
celebrated Chinese archer
TO IMPROVE HIS EYESIGHT
PINNED A FLEA TO THE WALL
AND GAZED AT IT WITHOUT
BLINKING EVERY WAKING
MOMENT FOR 3 YEARS!

THE **SHIP** THAT WAS WRECKED
ON EVERY VOYAGE!
THE "GEORGE F. WHITNEY"
A SCHOONER LAUNCHED IN 1871
WENT ONTO THE ROCKS AT SUGAR
ISLAND ON ITS MAIDEN VOYAGE
IT WAS REBUILT -AND WAS
WRECKED AT VERMILION, OHIO,
ON ITS SECOND VOYAGE—
REBUILT AGAIN IT SAILED INTO
A STORM ON LAKE MICHIGAN
AND VANISHED WITH ALL HANDS

THE **TURPEN BROTHERS**
ARE IDENTICAL
TWINS
-YET THEY
WERE BORN
ON DIFFERENT
DAYS AND IN
DIFFERENT
TOWNSHIPS

PARISIENNE WOMEN in the 19th century ACHIEVED THE BEAUTY OF EYE SHADOW BY *TATTOOING THEIR EYELIDS*

KERRIA JAPONICA
A JAPANESE ROSE *PRODUCES CHERRIES IN THE CENTER OF EACH BLOSSOM*

NORMAN S. BROCKWAY
(1841-1936)
FAMED RIFLE MAKER of Bellows Falls, Vt., WITH HIS LEG SUFFERING FROM GANGRENE, RODE THE FIRST TRAIN TO KEENE, N.H. TO HAVE HIS FOOT AMPUTATED— *THE SURGEON WAS CELEBRATING THE RAILROAD'S COMPLETION, SO BROCKWAY RETURNED HOME WITHOUT THE OPERATION—AND LIVED ANOTHER 70 YEARS*

THE CATHEDRAL OF PADERBORN in Germany WAS BUILT OVER THE SOURCE OF THE PADER RIVER —*WHICH FLOWS NOW FROM THE CATHEDRAL'S FOUNDATION*

THE EUROPEAN MUDFISH LAYS ITS EGGS IN THE SHELL OF A LIVING MUSSEL—*WHERE THEY HATCH*

CONSTANTIN MAUROCORDATO WAS CROWNED RULER OF Wallachia, Rumania, 5 TIMES AND *DETHRONED 5 TIMES*

THE GORGON SILVER COINS used in Macedonia 2,400 years ago FEATURED THE DISTORTED FACE OF A DEMON *TO FRIGHTEN OFF ROBBERS*

CHINESE MARINES SENT AGAINST THE MIGHT OF THE BRITISH NAVY IN THE SINO-ENGLISH WAR OF 1844 *WERE ARMED WITH MATCH-LOCK PISTOLS AND A TRIDENT AND MOUNTED ON INFLATED PIG SKINS*

THE 3,000 NATIVES of Orgossolo, Sardinia, SPEAK A LANGUAGE THAT IS UNKNOWN ANYWHERE ELSE IN THE WORLD—*EVEN IN OTHER PARTS OF SARDINIA*

LYCURGUS the Spartan lawmaker INCORPORATED IN THE CONSTITUTION OF SPARTA A PROVISION OBLIGING EVERY HUSBAND TO ARRANGE FOR A SUCCESSOR —*WHO WOULD TAKE HIS PLACE IF HIS WIFE BECAME A WIDOW*

GUILLOTINE MADE BY FRENCH PRISONERS in England *ENTIRELY FROM CHICKEN BONES AND FISH BONES* (1815)

THE MARSH SNAIL IS BORN ALIVE —*ALREADY IN ITS OWN SHELL*

THE SMALLEST BET PERMITTED IN THE COURT OF CATHERINE OF RUSSIA *WAS A GOBLET OF GOLDEN DUCATS EACH DUCAT WAS WORTH* $2.28

THE **CAVALRY** OF DJINGHIS KHAN COVERED VAST DISTANCES AT TREMENDOUS SPEED BECAUSE EACH MAN HAD 6 HORSES — *SO HE ALWAYS RODE A FRESH MOUNT AND LED 5 OTHERS*

THE CITY HALL of Oestrich, Germany, HAS A CHIMNEY SHAPED LIKE A HOUSE – A MINIATURE REPLICA OF THE HOME OF THE BUILDER *WHO USED THIS MEANS OF "SIGNING" HIS WORK*

A **LOCOMOTIVE**
EQUIPPED WITH A SNOW PLOW
TOOK 32 DAYS TO CLEAR THE
TRACKS OF THE SILVERTON R.R.
OF SNOW BETWEEN
Needleton and Silverton, Colo.
-A DISTANCE OF ONLY
12 MILES (April, 1932)

A **PAGAN ALTAR**
THE
REMAINS OF
AN ANCIENT
ROMAN
TEMPLE
WAS
EXCAVATED
-AND
STILL
STANDS-
IN THE
CHURCH
OF
STONE
(England)

LOUIS HENRI, PRINCE de CONDÉ
(1692-1740) of France
AFTER BEING BLINDED IN THE RIGHT
EYE IN A HUNTING ACCIDENT, BECAME
THE FATHER OF 12 CHILDREN
-EACH OF WHOM WAS BORN
BLIND IN THE RIGHT EYE

THE FLAG of SAUDI ARABIA IS THE ONLY NATIONAL EMBLEM THAT IS NEVER FLOWN AT HALF-MAST—LOWERING IT IS CONSIDERED A SIGN OF DISRESPECT TO THE DEITY

THE ISLAND OF THE DEAD
THE ISLAND OF ST. GEORGE IN THE ADRIATIC SEA SERVES THE TOWN OF PERAST, YUGOSLAVIA, *AS ITS CEMETERY*

THE MILK RUN!
A YOUTH of the Banna Tribe of Southern Ethiopia, TO BE CONSIDERED A MAN, MUST RUN ACROSS THE BACKS OF A HERD OF COWS AND MAKE A LEAP FROM THE GROUND ACROSS THE BACK OF THE LEAD COW—*WHOSE NAME HE THEN TAKES AS HIS OWN*

A **FIRE** LIT ON THIS ALTAR IN AN ANCIENT TEMPLE IN LUXOR, EGYPT, EXPANDED HOT AIR INSIDE THE ALTAR, WHICH FORCED WATER FROM A JAR INTO A BUCKET, THE ADDED WEIGHT CAUSING THE BUCKET TO PULL A ROPE — *WHICH IMPRESSED THOSE PRESENT BY CAUSING A DOOR TO SWING OPEN MYSTERIOUSLY*

"RIP ROWSER BILL" A DESPERADO WHO ARRIVED IN Oklahoma City, Okla., in 1889 TERRORIZED THE CITIZENRY BY ANNOUNCING HE HAD COME TO "START A NEW GRAVEYARD"— *HE KEPT HIS PROMISE BECAUSE HE WAS HANGED AS A RUSTLER AND HIS OWN GRAVE WAS THE FIRST IN THE NEW CEMETERY*

THE WATER BOATMAN an insect, SWIMS UPSIDE DOWN AND BREATHES FROM AIR BUBBLES ON ITS OWN BODY

POSTCARD MAILED IN Bridgewater, So. Dakota, ON AUGUST 4, 1939 AND DELIVERED TO ITS ADDRESSEE IN Boulder, Colorado, *24 YEARS LATER*

THE **HAMMER-HEAD BIRD** of South Africa
16 INCHES TALL, BUILDS A NEST **6 FEET IN DIAMETER** *THE NEST'S DOMED ROOF CAN SUPPORT THE WEIGHT OF A HEAVY MAN*

A *CHURCH* BUILT IN 1913, IN Grytviken, on So. Georgia Island IS THE MOST SOUTHERN CHURCH IN THE WORLD

DR. JOHN HUNTER (1728-1793) foremost English surgeon of his time REPEATEDLY WARNED HIS COLLEAGUES NEVER TO CONTRADICT HIM DURING A LECTURE— *CHALLENGED FOR THE FIRST TIME BY AN ASSOCIATE WHILE READING A PAPER* in St. George's Hospital, London, *DR. HUNTER CLUTCHED HIS CHEST AND FELL DEAD*

EUGENE LE ROY
(1836-1908) WHO BECAME A FAMOUS FRENCH AUTHOR, IN FULFILLMENT OF A PROMISE TO HIS MOTHER, WORKED AS A GOVERNMENT TAX COLLECTOR FOR 58 YEARS - AND DID NOT WRITE HIS FIRST BOOK UNTIL HE WAS 59 YEARS OF AGE

THE **OLDEST PARK** IN THE UNITED STATES
BOSTON COMMON, A 45-ACRE TRACT, PURCHASED IN 1634 AS A COW PASTURE, HAS BEEN A PARK FOR 324 YEARS

THE **OLD MAN**
NATURAL STONE FORMATION
Petrified Gardens, Saratoga Springs, N.Y.

BUNS MARKED WITH A CROSS WERE USED AND REVERED BY THE ANCIENT EGYPTIANS *THOUSANDS OF YEARS BEFORE CHRISTIANITY*

EGYPTIAN FARMERS DAILY CROSS the Nile *ASTRIDE A LOG* -WHICH THEY PADDLE WITH THEIR HANDS

THE CHURCH of ST. ANTHONY of PADUA in Moncucco, Italy, ORIGINALLY CONSTRUCTED IN LUGANO, SWITZERLAND, WAS DISMANTLED AND TRANSPORTED TO ITS PRESENT SITE *THROUGH ALPINE PASSES-A DISTANCE OF 60 MILES*

PHILIP LORD WHARTON (1613 -1696) AS BUTTONS ON HIS CLOTHING *ALWAYS USED DIAMONDS*

ASHIN a village in the Great Desert of Iran IS OCCUPIED ONLY DURING EACH FALL AND WINTER *BECAUSE ALL ITS INHABITANTS SPEND THE REMAINDER OF EACH YEAR WANDERING IN THE DESERT*

THE WOMAN WHO DROWNED ON DRY LAND Mrs. Richard Wald of Sycamore, Ill., DRANK 3 GALLONS OF WATER IN ONE HOUR *AND DIED OF DROWNING* (Jan. 1915)

MUSHROOM ROCK in Fobane Nek, Leribe, S. Africa, IS SO DELICATELY BALANCED THAT IT REVOLVES ON ITS BASE

A **TEMPLE** in Shensi, China, THAT IS VISITED BY NATIVES SEEKING RELIEF FROM ASTHMA BECAUSE THE STRUCTURE IS HALF BURIED BY SAND -WHICH HAS ALMOST CHOKED OFF ITS ONLY MEANS OF ENTRY

DR. CHARLES W. EKERMEYER (1857-1930) of Montgomery, Ohio, PRACTICED MEDICINE FOR 53 YEARS -AND NEVER ONCE SENT A PATIENT A BILL

"Kroumir" A PERSIAN CAT OWNED BY FRENCH JOURNALIST HENRI ROCHEFORT REFUSED TO LEAVE THE COFFIN OF HIS MASTER-TOOK NO FOOD OR WATER FOR 7 DAYS-AND FINALLY DIED BESIDE HIS GRAVE July 3-10, 1913

DINNER KNIVES
in the 19th century
AS A PRECAUTION
AGAINST THE HOST'S
FORGETTING TO SAY GRACE
WERE SOMETIMES ENGRAVED
WITH MUSICAL NOTES
AND A LATIN PRAYER

NAIL
USED IN THE
CONSTRUCTION OF
THE ROMAN FORT OF
SAALBURG, in the
Taunus Mountains
of Germany
-STILL IN GOOD
CONDITION
1,825 YEARS LATER

THE
**STRANGEST
FINANCIERS
IN THE
WORLD**
THE PAHARIS
of Naini Tai,
India,
farm laborers
NEVER
DRAW
THEIR
PAY
-LEAVING
IT
INSTEAD
WITH THEIR
EMPLOYERS
AT 25 PER CENT
INTEREST

WITHIN A FEW
YEARS THEY
USUALLY OWN
THE FARMS
AND THEIR
FORMER
BOSSES
ARE THEIR
LABORERS

THE RUINS
of the Church of Bailleul, France,
HAVE BEEN PRESERVED AS
A WAR MEMORIAL

THE **STRANGEST SUICIDE IN HISTORY!** DEWA AMMAJEE of Coorg, India, THE WIDOW OF A RAJAH DETERMINED TO FOLLOW HER HUSBAND IN DEATH *GROUND UP A 20-CARAT DIAMOND AND SWALLOWED ITS DUST!*

LYLE KOEHLER of Wisconsin State College, at La Crosse, Wis., READ **500** FULL-SIZED BOOKS LAST YEAR *COMPLETING 70 OF THEM IN A SINGLE MONTH*

A **ROW** of **ALMSHOUSES** in Droitwich, England, WERE BUILT BY HENRY COVENTRY IN 1686 WITH *$15,000 WON ON A SINGLE HORSE RACE*

EACH HOME of Calinga Tribesmen, in the Philippines, HAS IN FRONT OF IT A HIGH CHAIR ON WHICH THE BODY OF ITS OWNER IS PROPPED **SO HE CAN OBSERVE IN THE FIRST 24 HOURS AFTER HIS DEATH HOW HIS FAMILY IS RUNNING THE HOUSEHOLD**

SALLIE CREECH of Harlan County, Ky., CELEBRATED HER GOLDEN ANNIVERSARY IN 1916 *IN THE WEDDING GOWN IN WHICH SHE WAS MARRIED IN 1866*

JAILS for Indians of the Huastec Tribe of Mexico ARE NEVER LOCKED **BECAUSE THE PRISONERS ALWAYS TRAVEL HOME FOR MEALS**

LEWISTON A MAINE COMMUNITY OF 40,804 INHABITANTS HAD 468 DEATHS IN 1961 468 DEATHS IN 1962 468 DEATHS IN 1963

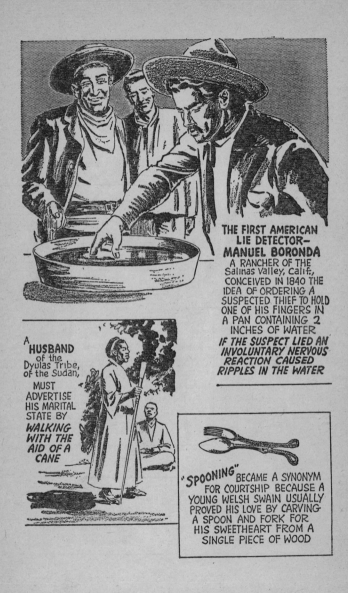

THE FIRST AMERICAN LIE DETECTOR— MANUEL BORONDA A RANCHER OF THE Salinas Valley, Calif., CONCEIVED IN 1840 THE IDEA OF ORDERING A SUSPECTED THIEF TO HOLD ONE OF HIS FINGERS IN A PAN CONTAINING 2 INCHES OF WATER *IF THE SUSPECT LIED AN INVOLUNTARY NERVOUS REACTION CAUSED RIPPLES IN THE WATER*

A **HUSBAND** of the Dyulas Tribe, of the Sudan, MUST ADVERTISE HIS MARITAL STATE BY *WALKING WITH THE AID OF A CANE*

"SPOONING" BECAME A SYNONYM FOR COURTSHIP BECAUSE A YOUNG WELSH SWAIN USUALLY PROVED HIS LOVE BY CARVING A SPOON AND FORK FOR HIS SWEETHEART FROM A SINGLE PIECE OF WOOD